A Lost Youth

I0117951

Abigal Mucheheti

chipmunkapublishing
the mental health publisher

Published by
Chipmunkapublishing

http://www.chipmunkapublishing.com

Copyright © Abigal Muchecheti 2013
ISBN   978-1-84991-972-2

Chipmunkapublishing gratefully acknowledge the support of Arts Council England.

Abigal Muchecheti

For Nigel and all the women who have gone through Female
Genital Mutilation

A Lost Youth

Chapter 1: IMMACULATE (MAKI)

It was November 17, 1982, the day of my twelfth birthday. Had I been from a normal family I would have been celebrating, expecting presents and maybe a birthday party with family and friends. But for me, turning twelve simply meant being married off to a promised husband.

It was as if my parents had been waiting for this day. They could have married me off before I turned twelve. After all, whether they sent me off at eleven or twelve, it would not matter. I would still have been underage – a child bride. It is not a common thing, but in remote parts of the country people can do anything and get away with it.

Apparently the traditional formalities had already taken place years back but I didn't remember. It had to be kept secret, though. That was why we had to move to the city immediately after getting married.

It was certainly not my intention to settle down at this age, but I had no say in the matter. Like all girls of my age, I had dreams. Some girls wanted to be teachers, nurses or scientists. Me, I wanted to be a pilot. Each time I looked in the sky and saw an aeroplane, I felt a pull. How would it feel to be in control of one of those, I had often asked my grandfather.

"That, Grandchild, is a mystery," he had said. "*Efulamachina*[1] is a great thing to have happened to human beings."

"Have you ever been in one?" I had asked him. "They say it is as is as comfortable as your own house. I don't believe it, though."

"These *Varungus*[2], what can they not do?" Grandfather had said. He had seen it all – the world wars and all the changes that had happened in my country from the days of colonialism to the war of independence – and he had survived to see what independence had done to the new corrupt government. He both admired and detested

---

[1] flying machine

[2] White people

technology. He had lost his job in one of the factories because his job could now be done by a machine.

"They will still come up with a new thing, wait and see," Grandfather added. "They will say an *efulamachina* can operate itself."

"I doubt it, Grandfather," I said. "It would be too risky. People would be scared. One would only be comfortable with humans up there operating the aeroplane in case things go wrong. I have not been in one of those, Grandfather, but one day I will," I told him.

"Where do you want to go, *Muzukuru, Hingirandi*[3]?" he asked me.

"Yes, Grandfather," I replied. "I do want to go to England. I want to do further studies at Cambridge or Oxford." I felt proud of myself, for I was only ten at the time, but I had it all planned.

Only two months after that conversation with Grandfather, he was dead. I now believe that if he had not died when I was ten, I would not have been married so young. He would not have let my father marry me off.

Grandfather was a poor man and left nothing to my father and his brothers, but he was a principled man, which is where he differed from my father. No disrespect, but I consider my father very weak when faced with challenges. He crumbles like a butterfly whenever there is a problem. He is easily influenced by other people. I have always admired men who fight for what they believe in, men with balls.

In those days I believed the sky was the limit to what I wanted. I read a lot of out-of-date newspapers that my father constantly brought to the house, and I knew that there were opportunities out there. I wanted to go far, I once told my mother.

"How about getting married?" she asked.

"I can always get married afterwards," I said.

I wanted to finish my education at one of the famous English universities, Cambridge or Oxford. That was the plan,

---

[3] Grandchild, England?

and I believed I could get a bursary from school and continue doing well. Of course, those were a young girl's daydreams.

I guess while I was dreaming about Cambridge and Oxford, some of my classmates were daydreaming about their crushes on boys. Not that I didn't have crushes on boys as well. I did admire smart boys. I was proud of my grades and life in general.

I was content, and the future looked promising. How could I have known what was waiting for me? I had seen classmates being married early, and I had never been sure whether they had wanted it or not. Some seemed to accept it as normal since they had seen sisters going through the same thing. There was no fighting spirit among the people.

I once asked a girl called Abbie why she didn't put up a fight against her impending marriage. I didn't know that one day I would be in the same situation.

"My parents know what's best for me Maki," Abbie had said.

Her sister Sofia had run away. She had been considered a rebel by the villagers, but she had said she would rather work in somebody's house as a maid than live a miserable life. She was untouchable now. She knew people in the city and told her parents that if they tried to force her into anything she didn't want, the police would be at their doorstep at the snap of her fingers. She had even written to the Ministry of Home Affairs with the help of one of her employers. They had got a response warning the villagers that they were being watched. She also wrote to the villagers threatening that she would take them to the human rights court.

People were scared at first, but eventually they thought Sofia was just seeking attention. Her concerns were mostly about the way girls were treated in the village. The main thing was female genital mutilation, as Sofia and her group called it. She said it was a crime against humanity. This made her the village's enemy.

With her maid's wages, Sofia managed to make herself look pretty. She even used skin-lightening products to change from the old Sofia. People thought she was doing this because she was attending meetings with some big people in the city. The villagers heard with interest through the grapevine of how Sofia transformed herself. She spoke calmly and with wisdom. She even visited with some of her European friends! This was unheard of – a woman challenging the status quo. Who did she think she was? Wait until someone gets her pregnant! Some people, though, admired her for her guts.

What was difficult, though, was the running away bit – where did one go when they got to the city? Sofia was lucky – she had the means: she had stolen from her parents the bus fare money and a couple of dollars for food. But because her parents were scared that Abbie would follow Sofia's example, Abbie was under surveillance. She had to do what her sister was supposed to do – get married.

A few girls offered resistance, but apart from running away there was nothing much they could do to avoid being married off. Even the village elders were accused of turning a blind eye when approached by individuals who questioned marrying off children. It was a family matter, the elders would say. They could not possibly intervene. After all, isn't it the parents who know what's good for their children? Surely they cannot have brought them into this world to cause them grief.

I had always considered such parents cruel, but would I really put my parents in that category? Were they not also victims in some ways?

"Victims? How can they be victims?" my brother said. "It is you and I who are victims, my dear sister." It was hard to think that way, but I had no choice but hate my parents for the time being.

"That is the best we can do," Aunt Meju said. "We can't afford to educate all twelve of you, and some compromise has to be made."

My aunt Meju, as we affectionately called her, had come all the way from Nyazura to help me accept what was going on. Her real English name was Marjorie, but the whole family called her Meju. Meju the troublemaker, always poking her nose in other people's business. She was much younger than my father and was always involved in family issues. My family was very old-fashioned, and problems were shared with the entire extended family.

My mother was fond of Aunt Meju, but I was always suspicious of her. She had married early and was now a successful businesswoman. No matter how things were with us, she never helped financially. She was full of advice and would bring gifts for us sometimes, but that is as far as she would go with the help. She was selfish.

"Why does she not pay my school fees at least?" I asked my mother. "We could always pay her back."

"We don't want to be in debt, *Mwanangu*[4]," my mother said.

"Your family is doing the best for you, you know," Meju said about my marriage. "That is the only way for you to get an education. I know you like school and you have dreams – the best thing for you is to do as you are told. Your parents really want to see the best out of you and you will make them proud."

"How can I make anyone proud when I am a child bride at twelve?" I asked. "By fifteen maybe I will be expected to have a baby, then two and three, and that will be the end of my big dream."

"Who said mothers don't go to school and leave their babies at home? Think, Maki," she said. "That man can do things for you if you are nice to him. Just be nice, do you hear me?"

"Who said girls have to be married off at twelve?" I said, walking up and down the room. "Do you know it is against the law? You are actually helping my parents break the law. If this comes out you will all be in trouble." I was hoping this would scare Meju a bit, but she was unmoved. She knew perfectly well what she was doing. I looked at her with eyes full of distaste.

"Don't look at me like that, child," she pleaded. "Come to your aunt. Oh, poor thing!"

I didn't move. I stood where I was, wishing the ground would just swallow me and protect me from what was happening to me.

At this point I hated Aunt Meju. I saw her as a she-devil. Why did my parents even bother bringing her to me? They had decided already and what I thought seemed not to matter. I sat there silently contemplating whether to kill myself or to run away. Neither idea was appealing. Killing myself –

---

[4] My Child

no way! Even if I wanted to, I seemed to be watched for twenty-four hours a day now. As for running away, not everyone was as fortunate as Abbie's sister Sofia. I had heard stories about young girls who found themselves being used as prostitutes in the city.

Pauline, one of the village girls, had run away from home a couple of years back and had become something of a heroine for doing it. No one knew exactly what she did while she was away. She had been fifteen, and wasn't running away from being married off. She was just bored with village life. When she came back she had not wanted to talk about how it was in the city. We guessed what must have happened, because she had come back pregnant.

A few years later, Pauline opened up. She had been taken by a man who kept her locked in a room. She was a sex slave. Different men were brought in to her day and night. She would have sex with each one of them for money, which all went to the man in charge. Pauline was not allowed to leave that room. Finally she managed to escape and came straight back to the village. She didn't want anybody else to make the same mistake. By the time she came back she was pregnant. She had no idea who the father was. She had been forced to have sex with men of different colours, and when she gave birth her baby was of mixed race. This raised eyebrows – but Pauline didn't care. She was back, and she had a healthy baby. People pointed fingers at her saying, "*Ane mwana mukaradhi,*[5]",but it didn't bother her.

I was not going to follow that route. I did not know anyone in the city, so running away was just impossible. I was stuck. I had to wait and see.

The waiting was hard. I felt like a prisoner waiting to be executed. Each time I heard the elders talking I thought maybe they had changed their minds. Luckily, schools were shut. How could I have faced all my friends at school? They all considered me inspirational. Who would not? I wrote English essays like a graduate would. These essays were read out to senior classes. I was called on to work out

---

[5] She has a mixed race child

mathematical equations for the senior grades, too. People were astonished.

"Where does it come from?" my brother once asked. "Is it all from that little head of yours? Unbelievable! You are truly a genius, a family gem. I would be happy to see you graduate – if it happens."

"What do you mean, 'if it happens'?" I asked. "It *will* happen. For my A Levels I want to do Chemistry, Physics and Mathematics." I had it all planned.

My brother never could hide his admiration and respect for me. But in this marriage matter he didn't know how to help me. I once caught him crying and asked him why. He said he was crying for me, for us as a family. I was touched. He knew what school meant for me and how good I was at it and he could not help me.

I had never seen him cry before. "Dear brother, cheer up," I told him. "It's not like I am dying. Remember, I will still be me, your sister. Please, you are breaking my heart, and if we both start crying it won't be good." I wanted to howl with him, to cry until all my tears had dried, but I was trying hard for the sake of my brother.

Now Aunt Meju was looking at me, waiting for me to continue our conversation. I wanted to smack her face. I wanted to make her feel the pain I was going through. At this point I looked at everyone around me with suspicion, except my elder brother.

I wanted to throw all of Aunt Meju's past gifts in her face. I was furious. How dare she say that marriage was the best thing for me! She was a hypocrite, I thought to myself. But much as I wanted to challenge Meju, I had to restrain myself. Having a row with her was believed to bring bad luck.

Outside, the day was lovely and bright, and the birds were singing as usual. I could hear children screaming as they played *pada*. I wished I was that young again. I would not be in this trouble.

The place where I grew up was not quite a village – it was really a settlement of people who seemed to have come from nowhere. The government tried to evict them as illegal settlers, but they were so stubborn that the government gave up. People in real villages, set up legally, used to refer to these people as 'squatters'. The settlers enjoyed being called squatters; it gave them an identity and culture of their own.

The real villagers actually admired the squatters, but there was always tension over grazing lands. Real villagers felt that if the squatters weren't there, there would be more grazing land for their cattle. There were cases of cows with broken limbs, acts of revenge by the squatters.

The squatter village was in the back of beyond, very desolate, and apart from the barking of dogs, birdsong, and peoples' voices there was not much to listen to. Cars were rare, and there were no buses. Most people had bicycles and scotch carts to transport their goods and to take sick people to the nearest hospital; some used donkeys. But if there were no heavy goods to carry, walking was the preferred means of transport. People would just walk for miles and miles.

Listening to the birds had made me think about all this, and took me out of my current plight for a little while. I tried to picture what life was like then. My mother had never said anything about how old she was when she got married. Judging by how many we were, and how young she still was, she must have married early. I could not embarrass her by asking about that.

"Auntie, how old were you when you got married? " I asked Meju, not because it was going to change things, but out of curiosity. Maybe I was hoping I could see things from her perspective.

"I was married when I was eighteen," Meju said. "In those days getting married in your twenties was seen as a bad thing. You had to be fresh blood and young. Girls in their twenties had no chance of becoming a wife. So whoever came your way in your teens, you would thank your stars." The only chance a girl in her twenties would have was a marriage to a man already married, sometimes to more than one wife. By the time Aunt Meju got married people had already started to make nasty comments about her. So she had been happy to be married at eighteen, and being the only wife had given her the opportunity to enjoy life.

I did not know her husband; he had passed away years earlier. Now I was curious about him. "So how old was your husband?" I asked. "I mean, was he an older man?"

"No, I was lucky," she replied. "He was only twenty-three, God rest his soul. He was a lovely man. Oh, we had such a great time together. I can see his smile now. We met at a dancing party," she reminisced, "and he was attracted to me at once. In those days I could dance like an angel, dancing for the Lord. I had many suitors, young and old, and I was lucky I could pick and choose."

"You see now why I am furious with all of you," I said to Aunt Meju. "You were allowed to choose whom you wanted to spend the rest of your life with, weren't you? Besides, he was not old enough to be your father, like mine is."

"I am really sorry that this is happening," Meju confessed, "but it is for your own sake. You will thank all of us one day. You should be proud of yourself for rescuing your family from poverty. You are being rescued as well. Imagine the luxury you will enjoy. That man is rich. I won't go into details now, but you will know on the day we leave you with your husband." I realised the reasons why I was being married off would change depending on who was talking to me.

I shuddered when she said 'husband'. What would I do with a husband, especially one who already had a wife and family? I was scared.

Still, I kept talking to Aunt Meju about what life had been like when she was a young girl. In those days people in the village used to do all sorts of things for entertainment. People got used to singing during the war, and in remote places like Nyazura people still sang and danced to the drum for entertainment. And they would go to the famous night dances, where women tried to show the men what they were made of, in the hope of getting a husband. Some got picked up by men for their singing; some, like Meju, for their dancing; and others for their beauty.

I tried to imagine what Meju would have been like at that age. She was a pretty woman that was quite clear. She had a reasonably big behind and a tiny waist, which made her look very sexy. Her long, black hair gave her an exotic look. Her teeth were as white as snow, and her smile was amazing. Men were always after her.

Meju had not been educated beyond secondary school. University was not really considered appropriate for women, since most got married and worked in the fields. Meju was lucky because her husband was a hard-working man and they managed to have a reasonably good lifestyle – in fact, many considered them posh. They had a lot of cows. They also kept chickens, and provided the whole area with chicken.

They were not an educated couple, but everyone thought they had 'brains'.

"Did many men go to school back then?" I asked Aunt Meju.

"Only a few," she replied. "Most did not get the opportunity. Besides, there was the war, and young men were exchanging their books for guns."

"At least they were given a chance to make their own decisions," I mumbled.

"Not really," said Meju. "There was always something to do: herding cattle, ploughing the field, maintaining the house. For some boys, school was the last thing on their mind. My Martin did not go to school," she went on, "but look at the type of life we had. He used to do piece jobs for the villagers and sometimes he would be gone for days because he could not finish his work and come back. He was good at thatching people's houses and got calls from all over the countryside."

I think Meju was trying to tell me that school alone is not enough for good life. Some might need both, but others might only need entrepreneurship. I believed in getting a good education for myself and seeing what was out there.

The first schools in the village were always empty. Teachers spoke to the villagers in the hope that they would send their children to school, but it was a waste of time. Books were a threat to locals. Nobody wanted to learn a new language – they were proud of their own language, and did not see the need to learn the "missus's language," as they called English. Rhodesia before independence was ruled by a minority of white individuals who derogated the native black population, so after independence people embraced their own language and culture.

My talk with Meju was coming to a close. Aunt Meju had done her best to cheer me up and to convince me that all that was being done was for a good cause. The marriage was settled. She was going to assist my mother in settling me down with my new family. I was to remember our conversation for years to come.

Chapter 2: IMMACULATE

Days before my marriage, I found it hard to fall asleep. This particular day, the smell of smoke and the hooting of an owl woke me from my deep slumber. It was dawn, and I had been having a nightmare. I dreamt a woman was about to stab me with a knife. I screamed and got up. I guess this was just me worrying about my relationship with the wife of G, the man I was going to marry. I needed the toilet, but my brother was sitting by the fire outside, and we did not use the pit latrine in the dark. I quickly went to the other side of the house to help myself. After that I went over to my brother and asked why he was not in bed.

"I am doing some thinking, sister," he said. That was worrying.

"But how are you managing with all that smoke?" I asked him. I could barely see him through the thick grey smoke. Dogs started barking, and I shivered. When I was younger, my brother used to say that if you are outside and suddenly hear dogs barking, they must have seen something, so run for your life. He used to scare me with stories of ghosts and vampires in the village. The barking dogs scared me now, so I told him, "I am going in; good luck with your fire." My eyes were full of tears from the smoke.

At the last minute, though, I decided to stay with my brother a while longer. Maybe he needed a shoulder to cry on, like I did. Something must be wrong – he would not be out this early for nothing.

"Which pile of firewood have you used?" I asked him. "From the smoke, I gather you have used the one that has not dried out. Take it out of the fire and use the pile I fetched yesterday. This smoke will wake the entire village."

Eventually we sorted out the fire. I was the fire expert in the family, the one who always got up early to light the fire and boil the water for all of us to use. There were times when I felt tired of it all. Work all the time, except when I was with my books.

"What is the matter?" I asked my brother again. "Tell me about it. I know you are worried about my going to this man, but surely this is not the reason you got up so early to sit by yourself?"

"I have messed up, sister," my brother finally confessed. "I got a girl pregnant. What am I going to give her? We can hardly manage as a family, and here I am bringing in another mouth to feed. What am I going to tell Baba? He will kill me." 'Baba' was what we called our father.

"You idiot!" I exclaimed. "When did this happen, and how far gone is she?" I did not know what to say. I had so many worries myself, but this was big. "Have you told Mother yet, or Meju?" I asked. "Maybe you should tell Meju about this pregnant girl first. She will not be impressed, but don't delay – you don't want Baba to hear it through the grapevine.". I was worried for my brother. There would be no more school for him – he would have to look for a job now, to look after his new family. I was angry with him, too, for being so careless. He should have known better, considering how poor we were.

I left my brother and went back to bed. My mind was going in all directions. I had my own life to worry about, but for everyone else life had to go on.

How could my brother be so selfish? I thought to myself...

I did have a party on my birthday, a marriage party disguised as a birthday party. Normally we would not and instead of enjoying I was angry. We didn't have any birthday celebrations in the village, so even the villagers might have been surprised by us having such a lavish party. People celebrated many things, including circumcision and initiation ceremonies, but not birthdays.

I had been dreading being a wife ever since the evening when I had overheard a clamour of voices on the subject. Having heard rumours about my marriage, I asked my mother why she was doing that to me.

"It is your father's idea, not mine," she told me. "I have tried again and again to talk sense to him, but he will not listen. We talked about this so many times." I could see tears in my mother's eyes.

So I went to my father. He was feared by everyone in my family, including me, but that did not stop me from approaching him.

I had practised my conversation with him beforehand and thought the best way to start was to attack him. *Don't let*

Abigal Muchecheti

him explain. Attack first, I thought to myself. If he blamed my mother, I would fire it back.

At first my father waved me away like a fly before I could even say anything. But, like a fly, I came back.

"Um, I wondered if I could have a word with you, Baba?" I said.

"What is it?" he snapped. "Don't you see I am busy?" That was a lie, of course. He was sitting and doing nothing. I knew he did not want to talk about the marriage, but I was not going to be discouraged by his attitude.

"About my marriage," I blurted out, "I am not going to do it, I swear to you. I will kill myself before you give me away to any man."

"Who do you think you are?" he fumed. "You do as you are told, girl. Nobody challenges my decisions in this house. Nobody. You will marry him whether you like it or not. You do exactly as I say! Is it your mother who is putting this poison into your head?" he demanded. "I know she is behind this. She is asking for trouble."

"Leave my mother out of this," I said. "My mother has done nothing wrong. I am not going to change my mind."

"One day I am going to beat you to a pulp," my father threatened. "You read a few books and you think you can rule the world? You think you are cleverer than the rest of us? It's that boy that you hang around with, isn't it?" he demanded.

So his accusations did not stop at my mother. Typical of my father, always pointing fingers at other people. He was referring to Norest, a good friend of mine. He was an orphan who had come to the village to live with an aunt. We soon became friends. He was an intelligent boy and we spent our time together doing school projects. We did arithmetic together, and discussed new discoveries together. If I read something he did not know, I would tell him, and vice versa. My father was against our friendship. He was sure it would lead to me getting pregnant.

"Leave Norest alone," I told him.

"Don't speak to me like that ever again!" my father barked. "Go back to your mother, and you are going to this man whether you like it or not. Get out of my sight! Now! "

I went off crying, but I knew that tears were not going to help. From what I could see every member of my family was going through some kind of stress. My mother was not

17

happy I was being married off to a man old enough to be my grandfather. As if this was not enough, I was also underage.

My father's bullying, I knew, hid the fact that he was angry with himself for having failed the family and letting me go. Much as he was keeping a brave face, the family knew he was hurting inside. In all this Meju became my parents' spokesperson. According to Meju, part of the marriage deal was that we would get food for the family whenever we didn't have enough – and we never had enough.

Meju had also told me that my mother had fought for another aspect to the deal. I was to get an education. How this was going to work my mother didn't know, but she had begged G to give me the one thing that was important to me, and G had agreed. According to aunt Meju, my mother had even taken my old school reports to show G. G was impressed and told my mother he was going to see what he could do, but I had my suspicions.

I knew that my mother loved me and that my brothers were fond of me – as the only girl, I was treated like a princess. However when I asked how the marriage deal was done, everyone became evasive. At this moment, though, I felt like a sacrificial lamb for the family I loved. A marriage of convenience. How was that going to work?

Chapter 3: IMMACULATE

I was the eighth of twelve children, and the only girl. That was an advantage for a few years after I was born, but turned into a nightmare when talk of marriage began. I was clever and admired by my family, including my father, who was not easy to please.

It seemed that the gods had been waiting for my birth and from then my fate had been sealed. My mother had had seven boys in a row before she had me. I was born pretty, with brown eyes and jet-black hair, which my mother took pleasure in plaiting every week. The rest of the family had Shona names only, but I was given an English name as well. My Shona name is Chioniso, and Immaculate is my English name. People called me Maki.

My mum recalls that I was tall and gangly from the start, and always smiling. I was thin, but I had full lips and a small nose – I think I was noticeable in a crowd, which gave me loads of confidence.

"You take after your grandmother," my mother told me. "She was a pretty woman, and you are just like her." I was not that interested in how I looked, but I liked it when people told me I was beautiful.

I always got very good grades and my family was so proud. My brothers, even those in grades above me, always came to me for answers. I was always reading, anything from old newspapers to any book I could lay my eyes on. My mother used to say I had better do well in school, because no man in his right mind would like books on the table instead of food.

I was considered spoiled-in many ways. Certainly my brothers used to think I was spoiled. But that was before things started going wrong. All I ever dreamed of was a good life.

My family was not rich, but we were happy. We had a small farm, just like all the squatters in the area. The area never had enough rain. My country is divided into regions according to how much rainfall each region gets. My village was in region five, the worst of them all. So although people worked hard, most of the crops died just after planting, and there was never enough food. Sometimes the villagers felt forsaken. This exacerbated the way in which families got rid of their children – or took care of them, as the parents wanted to believe. Girls were secretly married off, boys ended up herding cattle for richer families.

Life in the village was very communal. Everyone knew what every other family was doing. We grieved together, laughed together and even work in the fields was done, enjoyed and celebrated together.

Because of the inadequate crops from our subsistence farming, we got food supplements from the government. Even this was not enough, though. Sometimes the food only got to the families of the big shots. Ordinary people were left fighting – for nothing. Some of the food distribution meetings got so violent that some villagers were scared to attend. The food programme only catered for the 'real' villagers, since they were considered the legal residents, but the squatters had just as much need. They were not welcome at the meetings, which often led to fights. Food distribution meetings became war zones, with disastrous results for both sides. Food was often lost in the fights.

The government also introduced food for work programmes with the help of foreign organisations like Care International. Because one had to work, people were not as keen.

The year I was twelve, 1982, there was a severe drought throughout the country. Wells dried up; food was scarce everywhere. With such a big family, we were badly hit. Two of my brothers decided to leave home to be herd boys, and my parents had to let them go. There was no money for school fees. But even their going didn't ease the pressure for food. Something had to be done if the family was to survive...

The village was more of a bush than a place inhabited by people. It was surrounded by huge *msasa* and hibiscus trees, which acted as an enclosure and gave the village a unique character – but that did not save it from being slightly more backward than the rest of the country. There were very few schools, and most were sparsely attended.

I started school just before I was six. Children generally started at seven, and the head teacher was not keen on having me at school when I was so young. But I was tired of being at home and herding goats, and my mother was running out of things to teach me. In the end she said enough was enough and went to see the head teacher.

"She is too young," my father told her. "She will be playing while others are learning. Besides, she is mouthy and noisy. Mark my words, she will not last there. You don't want to embarrass us, do you?"

My mother paid no attention to him. She had bathed me that morning, rubbed my body with Vaseline, combed my long black hair, and told me to put on my socks and black tennis shoes. But my tennis shoes had holes in them, so I had to change into plastic shoes called 'Sandaks', which had been a gift from Meju. The village was hot, and wearing these shoes and socks was like putting your feet into a furnace. I hated them! They were ugly, with flat heels and laces. Most young people in the village referred to them as 'tractors'. When it was cold, they were cold, and when it was hot they were hot too.

"Mother, can I wear my tennis shoes with holes, please?" I begged. I did not want to be bullied because of my shoes. But my mother was adamant: Sandak shoes it had to be.

The head teacher was a serious-looking man called Mzondo. The last thing he wanted was an underage girl in one of his classes.

"That's not the way we do things here," he told my mother. My mother begged him and at least to give me a trial for a month. If I disappointed them, then they could send me home. Finally I was admitted into the first grade.

"You hear that?" my mother warned me. "If you misbehave, they will send you home and you will have to wait till you are seven like everybody else. The ball is in your court, child. Don't mess it up." And off she went home, leaving me at the mercy of bullies.

The other children all laughed at my shoes. How could a girl wear shoes like that? They were for men! By the time I got home my socks were in my pocket and I had hidden the 'tractor' shoes. That was the last time I ever wore them. The next day I went back to school wearing my tennis shoes with holes in the toes. I didn't bother with the socks.

The bullying over shoes stopped and moved on to the way I sucked my thumb. Why was I at school if I was still a baby? So, rather than be laughed at, I stopped doing some of the things I used to do.

The first month went by and I found myself still at school. I enjoyed school and read all the books I could get. (We did not have a library, so reading material was scarce.) I realized that I had a talent for words and picked things up easily.

Because we didn't have enough books for everyone, one person was always chosen to read to the class. After that we would answer questions written for us on the 'green board', as we called it. I was always chosen to read.

My parents soon realized what an avid reader I was. They were ashamed because they could not afford to buy me books. Then one day things changed. My parents had an idea – they set up an exchange programme with the local teachers, exchanging some of their important possessions in order to get me books to read. That worked for a while.

This was a big step considering that although they could read and write, none of my family was really educated. Understanding how important it was for me to read was the greatest thing they ever did for me. It always made me cry to realize how lucky I was to have the chance to have books to read. We used to keep chickens, but we never really had a chance to enjoy a meal of chicken stew and *sadza*[6]*, because our chickens disappeared into the book exchange programme.

So the teachers benefited by selling second-hand books to my father. But so did I. Who would have thought that, poor as we were and stuck as we were in the middle of the bush, I could grow up reading books like *The Grass Is Singing*, *To Kill a Mockingbird* and *Gulliver's Travels*? The teachers warned though that these books were beyond my age level and that I was too young to understand them, but I did, and I enjoyed them.

I became popular at school; people liked me. I also became one of the youngest storytellers in my village. My grandfather used to ask me to tell him about what I was

---

[6] South African staple food

reading. Although he had folktales to share with me, he enjoyed listening to my 'modern stories', as he called them. I remember him asking again and again about the Lilliputians in *Gulliver's Travels* and commenting on how clever they were. I also told him about Boo Radley in *To Kill a Mockingbird,* and my grandfather could not believe Atticus Finch could risk his reputation just to save a black man.

"Do you think men like Atticus really existed in the 1960s in America?" he asked again and again, until I wished I had not told him the story.

He could not hide his admiration of my ability to read a foreign language. "Do you mean to tell me that these books are written in the Queen's language?" he asked, amazed.

"Yes, Grandfather," I replied.

"You are good, Maki, you are good," he told me.

I also wrote good essays at school. I even once won the Commonwealth Essay competition with my essay 'Girl Child at Home'. I had written as if possessed, and the judges made me the overall regional winner.

Sometimes people asked me to read letters from their loved ones because they could not read nor write. I also wrote letters for others. Some of my classmates asked me to write essays for them in return for money or toys, but I never exchanged my knowledge for such things. I didn't want to abuse my knowledge.

I began turning some of the stories I read into songs. One that I remember very well was about Tim, a stray dog. When I recited it for my mother, she looked at me waving my hands in the air, and she cried.

Here is the story of Tim that made my mother cry:

"My name is Tim,
I am a stray dog.
I have no family...."

"Why are you crying, Mother?" I asked innocently.

She wiped her tears with the back of her hand and smiled. "Do another one for me, child. I like watching you do these things."

"I will do in Shona this time," I told her.

"Go on," my mother encouraged. I took my position in the middle of the room and sang:

"Ndege iyo
Ona Ndege iyo iri mudenga.

Inofamba yakatakura vanhu
Inotakurawo mbatya . . ."

I had always enjoyed the time I spent with my mother. It pained me to think all that would be history because of my impending marriage.

Disaster was always looming for my family, especially in 1982. My brother making a girl pregnant was terrible for my family. They thought they would have one less mouth to feed when I got married, but now I had been replaced. My parents were devastated, but there was nothing to do.

I became close to my brother's wife, Mavis, since neither of us was going to school. She was lucky she had married a man she really loved, unlike me. We soon realized we shared a love of books. We exchanged stories, and as she became heavily pregnant, we spent more time reading. Mavis had relatives in town who always sent her books, which I devoured within days. Mavis planned to go back to school after giving birth. We believed we were going to be great people.

"What do you find in these books, child?" Meju asked me one day. "Comfort and joy," I answered.

"No, call it running away from reality," she said. "I can see it in your eyes. Once you have a book in your hand, you are no longer here. Better start thinking about your husband, girl," she advised.

I knew I could go to the mansion, where G lived, for books, but I was scared. Meju had said to me, "It will soon be your house, so get used to it, girl." But I could not bring myself to go there – not now, when I knew that in a few weeks' time I would be his wife. I was scared and imagined all sorts of things. Besides, I was very shy now.

G did not come to our place, either, but he kept his word about not letting our family go hungry. I could see the food that his workers brought to us every week. This was done in secrecy, but I knew what was happening.

The food included sacks of sugar, flour, gallons of cooking oil, mealie meal and other delicacies we were not used to. Things started to get better now that we could all have three meals a day. The food was doing the family some good, it seemed. People seemed more cheerful now that their stomachs were being filled. We were also given proper soap, which was a big help with washing our clothes. Before, we had to rely on the strange soap my mother made from candles. It did not foam, which made it difficult to wash with the hard water we got from the river.

Now we had it all – including more money. It was the custom to pay a *roora*, a bride price – even for a child. My father used some of the money for my brothers' school fees. He also got himself a new suit and some shirts, and my mother got herself a dress and a blanket.

All my friends at school were quite sharp, and I learnt with regret that one of them, Jessie, was going to be married off to a man who already had two wives. It was a blow to all of us. Marrying off children seemed to be the fashionable thing in the early 1980s but it was done in secrecy.

Jessie was good at mathematics. She always wanted to be a mathematician, and I am sure she would have become one had she not been married off so young. My friends and I had met with her secretly and agreed to provide her with all the work we were given at school. It worked for a while, but before long we were caught out and were never allowed at her house again. To make matters worse, the other wives gave her a lot of work to stop her from studying. By the time she got home from herding cattle, she was too exhausted to study. Jessie ran away, but before long she went back. With no money and no relations in the city, she had not known what else to do.

Jessie's family belonged to the John the Baptist church, an apostolic church that was notorious for believing in polygamy. Most marriages were arranged between adult men and underage girls. Their reasons for arranging these early marriages ranged from making it easier to control the women to sheer poverty. Although the marriages were not legally registered, they were customarily recognized.

So Jessie was a victim of her religion. While we were still recovering from learning about her, another friend of mine, Eggie, disappeared. Rumour had it that she had been caught 'red-handed'. In the village, we all knew that all the John the Baptist Church girls were examined to see if they were still virgins. They said that God wanted all his flock to be pure. So every fortnight the girls under eighteen were taken to the river. There they were made to lie down one by one, legs apart, and have cold water splashed between their legs. If the water made a loud sound, then the girl's virginity was gone. If the women doing the job were in doubt they would use their fingers to check if the girls were still virgins. No parent wanted their girls to bring shame on the family, and those accused of having been 'spoiled' would have to be married off.

For some girls the forbidden fruit was always beckoning. Some deliberately slept with lovers from different churches, which angered the church elders. If these girls could not control themselves, then they needed a husband to be found for them.

But some were mistakenly accused of having lost their virginity when they had not. Once, when Eggie was in the queue to be examined, she had an altercation with one of the examining women. Inevitably she was found 'spoiled' and had to be married off. Eggie had never had sex, but that was the reason given for why she disappeared.

....
....

A few older members of the village remembered this when it happened. Maki was five when the marriage was officialised. It had taken the family a long time to know they had to compensate G's family with a bride. Misfortunes had been happening to Maki's family which made them desperate to do the sacrificial marriage. Maki's family had waited on each pregnancy as boys were born and when Maki was finally born her mother was not happy. She knew she was going to loose her only daughter. She tried to stop the marriage but with no success and when the traditional ceremony was done seven years ago when Maki was five, there was no going back. How could she fight against what was meant? There had been tension at first on both sides of the family. G who was chosen to receive the bride for the compensated family was up in arms. He considered the practice barbaric and abusive but his family insisted it had to be done and he was the chosen one. Beer had been brewed and a few close family members were invited to witness the marriage and Maki was to finally go to G 's family at twelve. What G would do with the bride was his choice. None of this was to be said to Maki until she was old enough to understand. At least there were other families in the village marrying off their children so Maki would not know exactly the circumstances surrounding her marriage to G for now at least. Her family only hoped she would understand and forgive them. A dead man's wife, who would understand that?

A Lost Youth

Chapter 4: IMMACULATE

Most of the village houses were made of poles and mud. But a few were not. One of those was the big two-storey house that belonged to G, the rich man of the village.

Nobody seemed to know when G had come to the village or how he had made his money. As we went about our day-to-day chores, people never really noticed him and his family. We belonged to different worlds.

As more of my family got word of my leaving home, I started to see G and his uncles around my house more frequently. I didn't pay attention to them at first. All I noticed were four grey haired good looking men. I learned later that G had been educated in what was then East Berlin. He was an engineering guru.

Women at the borehole used to gossip about him: he was the kind of man who would get whatever he wanted, they said, the sort that one would want to make love to all night. I dismissed it as just woman talk.

You could not miss him in a crowd. He always dressed in good-quality clothes, whereas villagers usually wore *mazitye*[7] donated from abroad. He was what every man wanted to be – smart, sophisticated and classy. His life in the village was well planned – exercise, for example. The villagers were not accustomed to exercise; people were healthy from the labouring in the farms and walking for long distances. Nobody ran. But G did, all the time. People would see him running around the village every morning.

"He is a modern man," people would say.

Others disagreed. "No, he is not. He is a fool."

"It's all those people he has killed coming back to him," another suggested, "troubling him, not letting him sleep."

"What does he want here anyway?" some people asked. "He is a stranger."

---

[7] Second hand clothes

"Let's be fair to the man," said someone else. "We are all strangers meeting in this place. He has as much right to be here as us."

"The only problem with him is he is a dreamer," said another man.

So G was unpopular with most men in the village. He was a challenge to their existence, a reminder that they were failures. Some men even beat their wives for mentioning G in their conversation.

G's wife was the opposite of him. She was kind of unspecial, humble and plain; in a room full of people you would not give her a second glance. Yet she had all the money.

She wasn't pretty, but she was very friendly. Though she wasn't originally local, her Shona was good. She spoke slowly, which made her seem wise – but this might just have been because she was not speaking her mother tongue.

In contrast to the poorly maintained *mud* houses in the rest of the village, G's was made of expensive bricks. People spoke about its grandeur. The house was also fenced, so we had to climb trees to see what it looked like.

He had a lot of servants and herd boys, and often had guests arriving in big four-by-fours. Everything about him was a bit mysterious. Locals addressed him as *Ishe*,[8] which he seemed to like. As it happens it was people like G who did well in the drought that left many people suffering.

As the drought began, we began to suffer. There were nights when no food touched our lips at all. We even ate roots that were potentially poisonous. Much as we loved each other, because we were a large family, we fought amongst ourselves for the little there was. We had to give priority to the younger ones, but since we were all born a year or so apart, we all felt we were young and needed food. We started relying on the food from the feeding point that was set up at school.

I was thin, but always cheerful, which made people admire me. I wished it was not happening, but I didn't

---

[8] King

complain. No one in my family complained —it would have been a waste of time. But people were angry. The villagers were angry with God for forsaking them, and angry with the squatters, who were blamed for anything bad.

This was long before the rumours of my being married off started, long before Aunt Meju was called in. Then things slowly started changing for my family. We started to have bread and butter for breakfast. Before, the only time we had good food was Christmas time, but now it was an everyday thing. I noticed that my father was dressing decently, and was spending time with the smartly dressed men who came from the big house. G 's uncles were always in the background. It was as if they wanted to make sure G does not pull out of the marriage deal. But my mother was not happy, and I had an ominous feeling. Something was wrong. But I had no time to think about it, because I was always thinking of my school work.

His name was Goredema, but when he went abroad he changed his name to Goetz. He insisted on being called G. A lot was said about him, but he never talked to people, which gave him an air of mystery.

At the time my marriage was arranged, I had not met G. He was like an invisible man, never seen in public places. One had to make an appointment to see him. If someone did go to him for help, he willingly gave. Those who were allowed into the walled house came back singing his praises. To some he was the village's Good Samaritan, but others saw him as greedy and selfish, and suspected him of dirty business. They enjoyed gossiping and invented stories about him, none of which were true. For example, they said he was a womanizer, which was why his wife had a permanently mournful face, even with all the money they had which was not true.

My visit to the house came about because of my aunt Meju and the need to formalize the relationship. All I was expected to do by Meju was to be a constant visitor to the library and take as many books as I wanted. That was very nice of him. I had never had the opportunity to have such a huge choice. The thought of seeing so many books was exhilarating.

When I arrived at the mansion, as all the villagers called it, with my mother, the servants were nice to me. Even his wife was pleasant to me, although begrudgingly.

The place was nicely maintained. The lawn was well cut and the flowers well trimmed. You could tell how much effort went into the upkeep of the house and grounds.

Inside, my mother and I were overwhelmed by what we saw. I cannot describe how beautiful this place was. I saw things there that I had never seen before in my life. The room we were taken to was expertly decorated, with curtains made of rich gold material. The sofas were made of leather, and there was an oak table in the middle of the room. The floor was covered with an expensive rug that matched the curtains. Who would have thought that someone in my village was living in such luxury?

As I sat there taking in everything, I noticed some stairs. Wondering how much more wealth I might find in the room they led to, I tiptoed down the stairs but the door was locked.

I was only half listening when the adults started talking, but then I heard my mother say, "She will do well at school – she is intelligent." This made me happy. I thought to myself, *If they are talking about me, then I will be fine.* None of the adults though included G.

Even so, I was not happy about the circumstances that had brought me here. I wanted to be back in the life I was used to, with my friends – my old life, where we were poor but happy.

I looked around, touching unfamiliar things just to see what they felt like. The adults' voices seemed far away, and I was lost in my own world, trying to absorb the environment – the sights, the smells. I noticed that the television was on – no one in the village had a television. *Sounds on Saturday* was on, a programme that featured western music. I kept my eyes averted to avoid looking at the half-naked dancers. I knew my mother was going to comment about that later because we were never allowed to look at magazines with pictures of half-naked women.

I left my mother chatting and sneaked into the study. What I saw took my breath away. The room was full of books, all neatly shelved in alphabetical order. I was mesmerized. In the centre of the room was a table with a tall black leather chair. I sat in it just to see what it was like – it was so comfortable that I didn't want to get up. And I could spin around in it! I kept spinning to see how far it could go. I had never seen a chair like that. In the village people sat on wooden chairs that were as hard as rocks.

To my right was a window. I looked out and saw an aeroplane with its vapour trail. I remembered my conversation with my grandfather about aeroplanes – *efulamachina*.

I did not stay at the window long. I felt ashamed for being in that house. It felt as if I was in a different world, not my world at all.

I turned back to the room, and began running my fingers over the edges of the books, just to enjoy the feel of them. I was excited. However, my thirst for books was not quenched yet, so I decided to sit down and read a little bit.

There were so many to choose from, books of different colours and different sizes. For some time I was torn between foreign and local authors. Eventually I picked one of my favourite books, *Waiting for the Rain* by Charles Mungoshi. I understood this book and enjoyed reading it.

While I sat there, I lost track of time. By the time I rushed to the sitting room, my mother had gone. I was to be taken home after supper. My mother had thrown me into the deep end.

Supper was great. I had never seen so much food. We all sat around a big dining table, and I was embarrassed because I could not use a knife and fork. The servants were giggling. But at home we always ate using our fingers, and I did not know any other way.

"You can use your hands, Immaculate," G 's wife said. "There is no need to be ashamed. That is how people have eaten since time began – our ancestors wanted to feel and enjoy what they were eating. So by all means do not force yourself to use cutlery." That was a relief!

After supper, G's wife went to her bedroom, and one of the girls called me upstairs to show me the rest of the house. All the rooms were neatly furnished, and all the furniture seemed to be new. The beds were all king-size. Compared with the single bed that I shared with my younger brother, they looked like heaven to me.

By the time I went home I was upset. How could people be living such a rich life in the village when the rest of the villagers were struggling for food? Where did this man get his money? Some would say it is through hard work, but others might say that it was through sheer manipulation of others. I was going to ask him when I got the chance.

"Ah, there you are!" said a deep, sonorous voice. I almost jumped. "Did I scare you? I am sorry, I didn't mean to. You are free to come anytime and get more books, Immaculate," he said. I didn't say anything. "I will drive you home now if you want me to," he told me, "but you are free to sleep over. You know that, don't you? This is your home now."

I froze. So this was it, our first face to face meeting without adults, I thought to myself. I had not been in a position to formally be introduced to G.

I was scared of this man. I had heard stories about him. Some people said he killed young children to enhance his riches. There is a belief that some medicine men can make people rich if they were willing to shed human blood, especially a child's. The killer would stay rich for as long as the child would have lived. He was accused of having done that.

All this was going through my mind as I came face to face with G. *What if he really is a murderer?* I thought to myself. *Or he could be a sadist, or a masochist. Who else would have a twelve-year-old wife?* I stood frozen to the spot, not knowing whether to run or scream.

In the end I stood my ground and looked up at him. He was rich, no doubt about that, but he was also a very good-looking man.

"Come," he said, giving me his hand. "Your poor mother will be worried. I thought I should let you enjoy the library for a while. Did you find what you wanted?"

I took his hand fearfully and we walked to his car. He helped me in and fastened my seat belt. After a while I managed to say, "Yes, sir." I didn't really want to pay him a visit again, but the idea of getting more books appealed to me.

"Come on, Immaculate," he said to me. "I have been told how clever you are. For a start you should stop calling me sir, all right? Please call me G. All my family do. It would be an insult if you insisted on calling me sir."

"Yes, sir," I said, and he laughed. His laughter was deep, like his voice.

"You are such a baby – a beautiful baby," G said, lifting my chin and sighing. "Don't worry, G will look after you," he assured me.

I was too young to make comparisons with other men, but I knew G was different. He was different from my teachers and all the other men I had come across. It is not our custom to call adults by their names. Even my mother addresses my father as Baba. Yet here was G, expecting me to call him by his first name.

'So Immaculate," he went on. "I know you are twelve, and you are the only girl in your family. Your other name is Chioniso, but your family prefers Maki. And I know that you love books. How am I doing?" he asked. "Tell me about your favourite food. I hope you liked the food today."

I was shocked. *How can he even ask me that*? I thought to myself. What did he mean, 'food'? *Sadza* and vegetables was the only food I knew. What I ate at his home was heavenly.

"Don't be shy," he coaxed. "Talk to me, Immaculate." But the more he insisted I talk, the more withdrawn I became.

He was driving slowly towards my house. I did not want to like this man, I kept on reminding myself. He was after all a parasite, feeding on young girls. I was suspicious of him, and kept thinking that he was only trying to be friendly so that he could get me. He must have been aware of how I was feeling, because he did not insist.

I was relieved when we finally got home. My mother was beside herself with fear and shame. She did not want to trouble him. She was going to send my brother to pick me up.

"Don't worry, *ambuya[9]*, it's a pleasure," he said. "Here are the books. She enjoyed the ride, didn't you, Immaculate?"

I was embarrassed to admit that I enjoyed his company – that was the last thing I wanted my mother to think. But G was different, and in a nice way.

---

[9] Mother in law

"Good night, all," he said. "I will see you all very soon." He waved and went back to his car. My husband was gone.

I stood by the door looking at the fading lights of his car, thinking about my future with this man. In the distance I could hear the drone of an aeroplane. I would never fly now, I thought to myself. How would I be able to live with someone I hated? I hated him for letting my parents do this to me. I hated him for being the person they picked to be my husband. I hated him for being who he was.

Later that night a message came from G that he was going away on business and would not be back for six months. I nearly jumped with joy. That meant I could go to school till then!

My family was worried – why had G decided to go away all of sudden? They hoped he would not change his mind over the next months. My mother was also scared that I might run away, and the longer the delay, the more likely that would happen. In the meantime, I had to go to school, otherwise my parents would have to explain my absence to the neighbours.

It was all good news for me. "Thank you, G," I said to myself.

Aunt Meju wanted to know every detail of my conversation with G. I told her about calling him G instead of sir, and she said I should do as I was told.

"So G it shall be," I said bravely.

"Don't be shy," Meju said. "After all, he is your husband."

Why a reasonable and educated man like G went for such an idea remained a mystery to me. But I put all that aside as I joined the other twelve-year-olds at school. My friends had no idea that I was carrying a secret.

Chapter 5: EGIFA

I am in truthfulness attempting to be cheerful about this whole topic, but I can't. I am most definitely a cheerful person. I can be agreeable too. But this time I am finding it difficult.

I will start with the time before I was born. I am not sure how my parents met, but my mother was a beautiful young lady then. She was still at school then and my father was a salesman for an Indian man who loved him like his own son. He had seen her when he travelled to Lusaka, Zambia, where my mother is from. Her looks and cheerfulness had attracted my father, who swore he would not let her out of his sight until he found out where she lived. He was as handsome as she was beautiful, and they fell head over heels in love. Mum dropped out of school, arrangements were made and within three months my parents were married. They were happy.

My mother left all her family in Lusaka and settled in Zimbabwe with my father. They always remind each other how intelligent my mum was and what a pity it was that she could not finish her studies. She tried to go back to school under the government's adult education scheme, but because of the family she could not cope.

Not only is she intelligent, my mum is clever and hard-working as well. My father was an active supporter of the war of liberation in the late 1970s. Like most women of her generation, she wanted to do things to please her husband, so she became active in cooking for the freedom fighters. As she was a foreigner, villagers respected her even more for helping with the fight. She is helpful, but unlike many other women of her generation, she is very independent and strong willed.

My father was lucky. He worked as a salesman and managed to buy a house in Kwekwe. His efforts to please his foreign wife had worked out well. But that was before he sold the house to move to the 'Promised Land' full of milk and honey – the squatters' campsite.

My mother had been against the idea from the start, but no one could stop my father once he set his mind on something. Unfortunately for the family, he had bought a big herd of cattle with the money from the sale of the house. During the drought the cattle had all died, and my parents were left with nothing.

Then there was me, Egifa. I was born clever. I had my mother's Zambian blood, and I was beautiful like her, and stubborn. My parents were happy.

Then my father decided to join the John the Baptist Church. What he saw in this church, I never found out. At first my mother did not want to go. She disliked the plain white garb, the bare feet and the shaved heads. But eventually she agreed. We all had to shave our heads and abide by the church rules.

One of the rules I found disgusting was the *zameni*, as they called it – the physical examination of girls to check whether they were still virgins. My mother objected – who would want their daughter to do go through that? –but I still had to take part. To instil fear in the young girls, it was done when all girls were together by the river.

A friend had once told me that she did have anal sex from time to time to avoid being caught. I could not bring myself to have sex at all – I was not ready. Besides, I was not in a relationship. But 1982, as it turned out, was not my year. One day, during the *zameni*, I was accused of having lost my virginity.

I was by nature argumentative, especially for what I believed in. "How can that be, when I have not slept with any man?" I asked the lady in charge.

"Well, you have been caught red-handed," the woman replied. "When the water was scooped between your legs it was clear you were not a virgin any more. You should be ashamed of yourself. What have you got to say for yourself, child?"

I wondered if this was to do with an argument I had had with one of the women or whether it was because of their dislike of my mother the foreigner. The previous week I had refused to have the *zameni* done because of my menstrual period, but the women had thought I was lying. They did not like my mother, and I suspected these women decided to spite my mother by suggesting I was messed up.

"Ha ha ha," one of the women laughed at me now. "Did you think we were not going to catch you?"

Back home I was livid. I knew I had not slept with anybody.

"So what now, Mother?" I asked, crying. "You know I would have told you if I had slept with anybody."

This was humiliating for the family. Everyone at church would think that I was a dirty little sex maniac, and the church elders would have to get me a husband. My parents had no say in this. Once it was made public that I had been found 'dirty', no man would want me.

"Mother, I am sure there are girls there who are still going to school even after sleeping with their boyfriends," I said, pleading. "Why can I not go to school too?"

But she could not do anything. Our lives were taken over by church people. My fate was sealed. Rumours began to circulate about me, and my classmates taunted me.

"So how wide is your vagina, Eggie?" they would yell. "As wide as a well!" they would chorus. Then they would laugh and run away. I felt humiliated and stopped going to school. I asked my mother if I could go to Zambia to live with her family, but organizing a journey like that needed money and time. Besides, my mother said it was too far away. I was her only child – what would she do without me?

"But Mother, I would be able to go to school in Zambia," I pointed out. "I could help you and Father once I get qualified." But she refused.

I had made up my mind. I was not going to let these people play around with my life as if it were a pair of dice. My vagina was not as wide as a well, and I knew what I wanted in life. I had to give it a try, even if that meant leaving the village by myself. I had to find the means.

In the end my mother wrote to her family in Zambia explaining what had happened. I was to go to Kitwe and stay there with my cousins. It was a long journey by train, but I had to go. It was not the ideal solution, but for the moment it was the best we could do.

The village had humiliated not only me, but my mother as well. She would be the subject of gossip for a while, and she would always be seen as a failure. I was determined to work hard to prove the village wrong.

A Lost Youth

Chapter 6: The Village Gossipers

Everything that was said about G was hearsay. He never confided in anyone, and he had no friends in the village. All his friends came from the city. He and his family had invaded the village like a foreigner, with no connection to the place, and he was a stranger to the villagers.

But things were said about him: He was everything that was evil. What sort of decent man would call himself G? It sounded like a bank robber's name! There was something creepy about him. Parents warned their children not to go anywhere near him, but he seemed to attract people anyway. Some people were fascinated by his car, or even his bicycle. He always had something different from the rest of the village.

G was born intelligent and handsome, and he became a master manipulator. He picked out those who would be most useful to him, then dumped them afterwards. He was also a detested man. Is that not what poor people do? They accuse those with money of making their millions through evil ways. According to those who claimed to know him, no god was sweeter or more praiseworthy to G than the god of money.

It was said that G had been educated in the then Soviet Union. Having been born fifty years back, he was lucky to have been educated at all. His education is said to have been an accident. His father was an accountant for a white farmer who was generous to his black workers. Because G's father had been loyal for a long time, the white farmer asked him what he really wanted for his children. G's father, foreseeing change in the near future, suggested sending his son abroad to study. The choice of where G was to go just came out of his father's mouth, and his employer did exactly what he asked. Off G was sent to the Soviet Union.

What he did there is a matter of secrecy, but he came back a polished man and a good businessman. He had enjoyed his studies and his time in the Soviet Union, and he had never come home to visit. This broke his mother's heart, and she died before he could make her proud. His father was not happy, but G was happy with himself.

He had contemplated staying abroad, but in the end he returned because he wanted to see his family. He also thought of the abundant business opportunities that would be available in Zimbabwe after the war.

By the time G came back, a lot had changed. Although the war was still going on, he made sure he remained neutral, not supporting either the freedom fighters, as they were called, or the Rhodesian forces. That's when his entrepreneurship began; it flourished into independence.

G had met his wife before he left for the Soviet Union. She lived near his home. It was said that he was not really in love with Maria, but had just wanted to please his parents. Unfortunately, she was madly in love with him. He had never taken Maria seriously and hoped she would give up and move on while he was away, but she had waited. He spent more than ten years in the Soviet Union, had different women every night and even wrote that she should move on, but to his annoyance Maria insisted on waiting.

G managed to pass his exams and get his degree in Engineering. Life had been sweet, but eventually he decided to go home. When he saw that Maria was still waiting for him, he felt too guilty to push her away, and he married her against his will.

He felt trapped, and spent a lot of time away from home. Maria remained faithful and loyal to him, gaining the respect of his family. But right from the start, G felt only hatred for his wife, they said. None of the things people talked about was true of G. People had to have something to talk about.

Chapter 7: MANYARA

My name is Manyara, which means 'the shy one' – but I am not a shy person. We were not originally from Zimbabwe. My parents came from Malawi just before I was born. In 1982, I was twelve years old.

Villagers saw us as strange because we still followed certain Malawian customs. I did not know much about these customs, but my mother promised me that everything would be clear once I came of age.

I was born into a poor family, but I didn't mind. I always enjoyed life – and everyone in my village was poor.

My father had four wives, and my mother was the last. My mother had six children; I was the third one. I had two older brothers and three younger sisters, who looked up to me for advice, even though I had feet of clay. I could never give good advice to anybody.

We were a big family, and when I was twelve I didn't know if I would finish school – but that didn't bother me. I admired people who were good at school, but it wasn't for me. I was always getting bad grades.

I think my dislike of school stemmed from teachers making me do things I didn't want to do. All the time it was "Manyara, stop that! Manyara, where is your homework? Manyara..." Why wouldn't they leave me alone?

At home, Mama shouted at me too. "You are lazy and dull in class! What are you good at? What am I going to do with you, Manyara?"

Not that I was expected to do much – in the 1980s most women were expected to be prepared for marriage. They were to be possessed, have children and work in the fields. So education was not really a priority for most families with girl children.

Most of the women I saw as I was growing up were praised for being hard workers. They worked all day, mainly tending the fields, herding cattle and running the house. We in the village rarely heard about women who had achieved great things. I was not going to be different from the rest of the village women. What was the point? We were a happy community with the way things were.

I was waiting anxiously for someone to ask for my hand in marriage, but nobody seemed to be interested. My half-sisters had not been lucky, either. We were all still at home. Most people considered our customs strange – after all, I was from a foreign land and from a family that practised Nyau dances. We were ridiculed. I had no chance of getting a husband in these circumstances.

Nyau dancing originated in Malawi. My father and brothers did these dances as part of our special ceremonies. At these ceremonial gatherings the dancers, who are only male, take the form of an animal to communicate messages from the ancestors. They disguise themselves with masks and costumes so they are unrecognizable. Sometimes dancers may also kidnap people and do other mischievous stuff to extort money.

My brothers used to leave school early just to be with other Nyau dancers. As men they were supposed to carry the culture and pass it on to the next generation. Unfortunately they became unpopular at school for being different.

We all enjoyed watching the Nyau dancers, and we enjoyed the air of mystery they gave us. But they made us feared by others. I had the feeling our culture scared suitors away.

I was one of those people who talk a lot. I didn't talk sense, but I just couldn't shut my mouth. I got into trouble at school and at home because of this. I also questioned things until I got satisfying answers.

One thing I was good at, though, was dressing up and make-up. No one else my age group did make-up as well as I did. All my pocket money went on make-up. I could not believe its magic power to transform a simple village girl like me into a sophisticated woman.

At times, not having roots in Zimbabwe made it difficult for us to live in the village. We had to keep to ourselves sometimes, especially during circumcision ceremonies. We had to ask to be excused from lessons, and we would sometimes be gone for weeks.

When I turned twelve, I knew that my circumcision would be soon and I hated the idea. Mother kept telling me, "You will soon be a woman." Because we were not in Malawi, it was difficult to do the circumcision as it is done there. For us kids who had never been to Malawi, though, this didn't matter. All we wanted was to have it over and done with.

I knew it would be my turn to go through the procedure and enter womanhood soon – then, hopefully, I would find Mr Right. The ceremony would be proof that I was ready for a man.

I had no idea of what exactly was in store for me. Pain yes but not what I went through. A group of us were all to travel out to the bush, where no one would see what was happening. We were to take enough clothes for a couple of weeks, and when we came back to the village we would be new and ready for the battles to come.

The initiation period did not only involve circumcision. It also included being taught how to keep a man happy in bed, and demonstrations were carried out with real men. It was the woman's responsibility to make sure that her husband enjoyed sex. If women did things properly, their men would not go running around looking for mistresses. There was no scientific proof of that, of course, but these women believed in what they taught.

From the start, I had been dreading the day. We left on a Friday night, and for the next month there was lesson after lesson, even on things that we knew, like cooking and washing ourselves.

"Don't just pour water between your legs," we were told. "Make sure you wash yourself clean, especially your female parts. No man wants to go near a woman who reeks."

Gone were the days of being shy. We were all women now, and most of the teaching was done practically. What I found distressing was the demonstration on sex. We were told that we had to keep our backs in the air, because once the back touched the bed, the man would not be satisfied. You had to keep him up until he released the semen. I could not help but let my back touch the surface. The whole business with these women was humiliating to me and the other girls.

"Up, up!" the lady in charge barked. "No man wants a lazy wife in bed!" In the end they had to put thorns under our backs, so that if we let our backs down they would touch the thorns and get hurt. I wondered how many people actually had sex in the way we were taught. I suddenly understood why this custom was kept secret – it was torture!

"Do you actually do that with your husband?" I asked Njaidza, one of the teachers.

"Manyara, be quiet," she snapped at me. "I will tell your mother how disrespectful you are!"

I did as I was told and kept quiet, but could not stop wondering if there was any point to what we were doing. To me it seemed too much of a hassle, all in the name of sex. I looked around to see if the other girls felt the same, but nobody seemed to share my views. In the end I told myself that there were probably millions who had gone through what I was going through now. Wherever they were, maybe they were happy.

I wanted to go home. The rumour was that we would all leave together after having been circumcised. No one was allowed to leave before the twenty-eight days were up, and some had to stay longer if there were complications. After that we were to stay at home until we healed. They wanted us to do the training first because after the circumcision we would have lost blood and would be too weak for such exercise.

Finally the day we were all waiting for arrived – the circumcision. I was hoping they would start the circumcision with me. I had heard a lot about circumcision and wanted it done and over with. I wanted to run away. I had heard of girls who had attempted to run away from initiation ceremonies, but none had succeeded. The women in charge were as sharp as the instruments they were using. They would not let any individual tarnish their success records. I knew I was not going to succeed, but there was no harm in trying. I wrote to my friend Maki about my planned escape.

Dear Maki,

You know how much I hate this, Maki. I want to try and run away. Call it impulsive, but I have to try. The weird thing is I do not know how to get home. But as long as I get back to civilization I will be safe. Pray for me, Maki. I hope I make it. You know I am not as good as you in these things. I wish you were here to help me.

Missing you, Maki, and wish me luck,
Your friend,
Manyara

It was only a wish, because I did not succeed.

Before leaving for the circumcision I had asked my mother many times, "Why are we still doing these things?"

Locals did not understand why we circumcised women, and people at school laughed at us. My mother gave me a lecture I could not forget on the history of circumcision and why my ancestors had practised it.

For generations, circumcision had been done to both girls and boys. For girls, the procedure varied from region to region, but mostly it was the removal of the clitoris. The clitoris was seen as dirty, and it would stop a woman from enjoying sex. It was also believed that humans are born bisexual and removing the clitoris gave girls their gender role in the community. Having a clitoris could lead to nervousness and even lesbianism, so it had to be removed. In some communities, it was thought that if a man's penis touched a clitoris, the man would die.

There is no way this can be true, I thought to myself. *If women are born with a clitoris, how can it be such a poisonous thing? Surely this is an attack on women.*

"If all that is true," I said to my mother, "why is it that some people don't do circumcision? Do you actually know anyone who died from his penis touching a clitoris?"

"I know of children born dead because their heads had touched evil clitorises," she replied.

"How do you know it was because of the clitoris?" I asked. "What if there was some other problem in the birthing process, for example?"

She had no answer for that. "Sometimes you shouldn't question things. Accept things the way they are, or else you will be forever searching," my mother said.

How ignorant and old-fashioned! I thought to myself. I knew I was dull in class, but I was always after answers. The circumcision theory did not make sense to me. If all that was true, why wasn't everyone doing it?

"Parents know what is best for their children, Manyara," my mother told me. "We would not do anything to hurt you. Take it with pride, child. We have all been there."

"That still does not make it right, Mother," I insisted. "I still think there is no justification for doing this."

"Manyara, learn to respect your mother," she told me. "This is our culture, and we will be passing it on to you – and so you shall pass it on to your children."

"From what I have heard I don't think I will have my children circumcised," I said. "It's like taking off your finger. If

God created me with a clitoris, how can it be such a bad thing? "

"If you don't have your children circumcised, they will bring shame to you, they will cheat on their husbands and you will be forever unhappy," my mother warned. I realized there was no point arguing with her.

My friend Immaculate from the squatter camp had told me they didn't do these things. Why did we have to be so different from others? I hoped I wouldn't have complications.

Secret as the ceremony was, stories were heard. One day just before we left for the event, I eavesdropped on a conversation between my mother and her friend Maggie. Her daughter Ruvimbo had problems after her circumcision. She was not healing and was having difficulty passing urine.

"Do you think she will be all right?" Maggie asked my mother.

"Is she keeping the cut clean?" my mother asked. "Maybe you should talk to Njaidza about it."

"You know how Njaidza is," Maggie replied. "She will say that she did the job well and that whatever is happening is my daughter's fault. I don't want to see my daughter uncomfortable, that's all. I just hope she will get a good husband after all this trouble."

Ruvimbo went through hell. Her cut did not heal well, and she developed an abscess. This led to many problems, especially with passing urine and menstrual blood. Walking was a bit of a challenge, too. I heard that Ruvimbo had to wash her private parts with salty water, and she got some powder from Njaidza. There was no mention of hospital.

Ruvimbo became withdrawn from everything that used to matter to her. She did not go out much, and my mother asked me to go and chat with her. Mostly she talked about wanting to kill herself.

"There is no point in living now, is there?" she said. "I won't be a proper woman. What will I tell my husband? I might as well just put an end to the whole thing."

I did not know what to say. I had heard a similar conversation with my mother, but she had just said that that was what a woman had to go through. Endurance was the key.

Neither Ruvimbo nor I understood why we had to be circumcised. Why were we treated differently from other girls?

I tried to make light of the situation. "They tell us that we have to have this done because an unmodified clitoris can lead to masturbation and lesbianism! Do you masturbate?"

She giggled. "Why should I?" she asked. We looked at each other and laughed. Finally I had managed to make her laugh but for me my turn with the butcheress was yet to come.

"It's all lies," I said. "That's just what they say to make us accept it."

"Maybe it's true, Manyara," Ruvimbo said. "We would never know, would we?"

"Do you fancy me, or any girl?" I asked her.

"Manyara, don't be silly," she replied. "I prefer penises, just as you do!" We both giggled.

After talking to Ruvimbo, I decided to write a letter to Immaculate and let her know what was going on. Since she had been whisked away by her knight in shining armour, I had not had the chance to talk to her. It sounds peculiar that I thought of G as a knight, considering his age, but Immaculate was doing well. She was going to school, which is what she wanted. The letter I wrote was very simple:

Dear Maki,

It was with great sadness that I learnt of your marriage to G. I don't know whether you are happy or not, but I am glad you are going to school. I did not like school as much as you did and I had to drop out, Maki, after the circumcision, which I am now happy to call female genital mutilation. I had a bit of drama with that old witch Njaidza. As you know, I tried to run away, but I was caught after a few hours, and the women were ready for me. I was rude to Njaidza and I think she hated me. I now understand why there have been people against this process. I felt humiliated. Afterwards, people talked behind my back and I could not carry on with school.

I am not happy at all, Maki. I wish there was something we could do as a community to put away such evil. Oh, Maki, I wish you were here. The whole thing was painful and I still have not recovered. To make matters worse, Ruvimbo, if you remember her from school, can't even walk after her female genital mutilation. She is so hurt she wants to commit suicide.

I am going to make my parents pay, though. I thought you would like to know that I am dating this guy, Alec. He is gorgeous. We are not having sex yet but we will once I heal. I have given up being careful. I know you would say that I should be on the pill, but no. I want to reward them with a bastard. So much for the family name.

My mother is calling me now, so I have to go.

I miss you, Maki. Please come to visit us.

Your friend,

Manyara

Chapter 8: MAKANDIDA

In the beginning it was just bush. No farmers, white or black, had wanted to farm there. It was hot, mosquito- and tsetse-infested and very dry. Only wild animals survived, and that was with difficulty.

Just after independence the new government embarked on resettling people in a bid to empower black people. After all, it was land that people had fought for. Throwing all caution to the wind, my father left his job to move to this new government experiment.

As far as I remember, the village became a melting pot for different tribes. People from different cultures came over, and in the end we were united by our desire to farm. As people mingled, numerous issues came to light, harmful traditional and religious practices that would affect me as well. These included female genital mutilation; virginity testing; forced marriages; victimization and burning of women who were so-called witches; dry sex, which entailed women applying douches to the vagina prior to sex to make it dry, supposedly to increase male sexual pleasure; and religious sects that did not believe in vaccinating their kids. I could write about all the injustices I witnessed, but this story is about me and my girlfriends from school, and how some of these things affected us.

As we settled down, it was interesting to see that although most people were very poor, there were a few families who were very rich. There was one person in particular who was rarely seen. His name was G. He had a big two-storey house, a big herd of cattle, and a lot more than ordinary villagers. While most of the villagers were using traditional farming methods, his was done the modern way. His farm was fenced, and you couldn't see anything inside.

G was such an exotic figure but people detested him. He was like fish among human beings. The good thing is he was a rich fish, and the bad thing is he was a dish. He was the one every woman in the village gossiped about when they were being naughty. I would not have minded having him as a husband if he didn't already have a wife and was my age.

There were only thirty-three families in the entire village. There was not much government aid, but with G's help, the village had built a school, a supermarket and a clinic.

Surrounding the village was a river where we used to go and swim. It was during swimming that I met a girl from the squatters' campsite. Her name was Immaculate. She was also known as Chioniso, but her friends called her Maki. The squatters were not real villagers like us and had no farming obligation to fulfil. They tried hard to be organized like a proper village, but nobody took them seriously. They were squatters, after all, and we had all witnessed the battle they had fought with the government. Some lost property, and their houses were burned, but they would just build them again. For them it was easier to put up a new house than to move away from the area. They felt they had the same rights as the rest of the village people. After all, the war of independence meant independence and freedom for everyone.

The rich had privileges that the poor couldn't dream of. Some families sent their kids to work for richer families so they could pay their school fees. I wanted to do the same when things started getting tough for my parents, but they wanted to protect me. Protect me from what? I wondered.

"We want to protect you from some village men who cannot resist young brides, especially in the face of crisis," my mother said. "There are evil men out there waiting to pounce on innocent twelve-year-olds."

"Yes," my father added, unnecessarily. "We have to protect our children." He always repeated anything that my mother considered important.

My father was a very soft, quiet man. He was polite to everyone. For him the most important things for us now were school and church. We had to go to church every Sunday. While other men sang loudly, clapped and danced to the songs, my father sang seriously, without moving. People thought he was too serious for life.

"Thank God you don't take after your father," my friends used to say to me.

People thought my mother was the man of the house. My father could not do anything without asking my mother first.

That was my family.

Chapter 9: IMMACULATE

I was enjoying the time I had at school with my friends. I had no idea what was going to happen to me after I joined G's family. Was I going to continue with school or not?

"It will all depend on your husband, child," Meju had said. "You will do as you are told."

One day after school, my mother had sat me down and talked about part of the marriage deal they had struck with the old man. It had not been what my mother wanted. She wanted me to be a free woman and to follow my dreams. Because I was the only girl and more intelligent than my brothers, she had hoped that one day I would be able to go places as I had always wanted. So, as the last resort, my mother had begged G to let me go to school.

"*Mukwasha*[10], I beg you," she pleaded with him, "nothing is more important to my girl than school. Please give her a chance."

"We will see what we can do," G had replied..

"Please," my mother said again.

"Okay, *ambuya,*[11]" he said at last. "But she might have to go away to boarding school."

That had given my mother some hope. Boarding school would not be a bad idea. At least I would be away from G's wife and kids. Still my mother did not know how far things would go for me.

My mother could not escape the fact that I was being married off to a man who already had a family. If G was an unmarried man, it might have not have been as bad. As it was now, things could go wrong. Nobody knew how his wife would take it. In the air there was this cloud of uncertainty and mistrust and I suspected there was something I was not being told.

From what my mother had said, G wanted another wife so that he could have a male child. His wife had given

---

[10] Son in law

[11] Mother in law

him girls only, and that was not good enough. I was expected to bring the joy of a baby boy into G's life. That was a surprise because there were so far different versions to why I was getting married depending on who was talking to me. I was now convinced that the marriage deal was more than what it seemed and I became more and more curious but not much came my way. I had to wait for when the truth would be revealed.

"We will have to see, won't we?" I said to Meju.

"Women are there to make their husbands happy," my aunt cautioned me. "Don't let us down, Maki. The blame will be on us for not raising you properly, don't forget that."

The bad thing about Aunt Meju was that she thought she knew everything there was to know in the world. She never questioned the logic of things. Her attitude of "I saw the sun before you, so I know it all" was what made us clash all the time. She was not only old-fashioned but narrow-minded as well. Yet she was always there for the family.

G was an educated man, so why he was doing something so traditional I never could understand.

"Education has nothing to do with it," Meju said. "Who wouldn't want a beautiful young bride when he is having midlife crisis? People have always done it, all over the world."

"I don't know much about the world," I replied, "but I do know that being forced to marry at twelve is wrong. How do you justify that?"

"Stop pretending to be cleverer than you are," Meju told me. "You will never get answers to all your questions. Questions, questions, are all that come out of your mouth. I would shut it if I were you."

Chapter 10: NJAIDZA

They all came to me with woman problems, everything to do with the female body, from circumcision to giving birth. In the village they gave me the nickname 'the butcheress' because I was the one in charge of the circumcision and initiation. It is something I had been doing since I was in my thirties. In 1982 I was fifty-five, and I had been doing my job well. There were fewer deaths than before and people still came to me secretly with their young ones.

I enjoyed doing it. To me circumcision can be compared to a new birth. It is a public recognition that the individual has become an adult. The removal of flesh is a symbol that the stage of childhood has passed and there is no going back. The physical mark during initiation is painful in order to encourage endurance. This prepares the initiates for the hardships to come and helps them to control their emotions. Let's face it, life is full of challenges. Unfortunately, the rest of the world does not see it this way. They don't understand, and that makes me angry. It is our culture, and I am proud to have been part of it.

I am one of those women born intelligent. I did not get formal education but in the 1980s I lived like a queen. Besides being in charge of the initiation ceremony and the circumcision, for which the parents of the initiates paid me well, I also ran a women's clinic at home.

Life had not been rosy for me in the past. I got married at twenty – I waited as long as possible, because I wanted to get the right man. Before that, I worked at a farm harvesting tobacco. Then I met my husband, Samuel. He was a village police officer. Not the same as a real police officer – in those days there were few black policemen – but all the same, he was paid for his job by the government. We fell in love immediately, and I got pregnant before we were married. We had a simple, traditional wedding. I borrowed a white dress from a friend, and the local priest performed the ceremony.

Life was good – until my husband was killed in an attack on an attempted robbery at another farm. Then things changed. I had no money to look after my two children. I was prepared to work hard to support them, but then a cholera outbreak took them from me.

That was the final straw. I had a mental breakdown and moved from village to village, not knowing what I was looking for. My life was gone. When I came here, I settled at the very end part of the village. It wasn't difficult to find someone to build a small hut for me.

The cholera that had killed my children had spared me, and I had to believe that I had survived for a purpose. I was not going to let my family down. I was going to fight to survive, and I made it a point to mix with the locals.

The first thing I did was open my clinic for women who were having trouble getting pregnant and giving birth. I was not trained, but I knew that I could help women to give birth naturally at home. I know that I was good at it – I have the evidence in the form of letters from clients thanking me for a job well done. One of the letters was from a woman who had been having one miscarriage after another. I helped her, and in the end she gave birth to a healthy baby boy. The letter read:

Dear Njaidza,

I am pleased to let you know that thanks to you I was blessed with a baby boy last week. As a token of appreciation I have enclosed a cheque of $2000 for you to spend. I promise we will also visit so that you can see the baby.

Thank you very much,

Amberleigh

It was a dangerous job, but letters like these made it worthwhile. I used the money to have a big house built, with a communal kitchen and cubicles so that the women who came to my clinic could have some privacy.

The health care system in this country does not allow free treatment. People have to pay for hospital care, even to give birth. If one does not pay, they are detained, all the while running up a bigger bill. As a result most people just don't go to the hospital.

That is why so many women came to me. Not that I treated them for nothing, but they could pay me in kind, with grain, livestock, clothing or anything.

Not all of my patients were poor. There were some who were rich but did not like giving birth in hospitals or were worried about being drugged. They preferred Njaidza's drug-free, natural way. Some of these women came from far away.

I also gave traditional medicines to women who desperately wanted children, or those with threatened miscarriages. Most of the time the medicine worked, and the women went away happy – and happy to let others know what I could do. So here I was, making money and helping people in need.

My work had its complications, though. It was a challenge to help women give birth without modern equipment. I tried my best to save lives, but some women died in childbirth due to complications. But it was all part of nature.

The older women were not so much of a problem, as they could handle many of the complications. The newly married twelve-year-old girls were much more difficult, and they had so many complications, from breech births to prolonged or obstructed labour. Problems in labour sometimes led to vital tissue dying, and eventually a hole, or fistula, in the vagina or rectum. That was a terrible situation, and no roots from Njaidza could help. After the birth the mother was left unable to control the leakage of urine or faeces through the fistula. That was the worst situation I ever witnessed with the young mothers in my twenty-five years as *VaNyamukuta*, a traditional midwife. The condition makes personal hygiene very difficult, as the woman is constantly soiled.

I was sometimes called out to try and explain to husbands why they should accept their wives back after this ordeal. Most husbands did not want anything to do with their wives once they had a fistula. Besides being rejected by their husbands, the women were stigmatized in the community and shunned by their families, which made them severely depressed. Some even died.

It was not my fault. Some of these girls are just not strong enough to sustain the pressure of the birthing process, especially at that young age. It was heartbreaking to see some young mothers rejecting their newborn babies after going through this terrible ordeal. All I could do was try to talk to them. But it was not my fault that they got pregnant when their bodies weren't ready for it. At the end of the day, I was just doing a job.

Unfortunately, often the hospitals couldn't deal with these complications, and even if they could, most people could not afford them. I couldn't understand why the hospitals were there in the first place, if they weren't available to people in need.

Some people thought I was heartless, but all I did was help women give birth. I had no children after I lost mine to cholera, and it pained me to see young mothers giving birth to stillborn babies. Death is painful for everyone, but it must have been awful for these young mothers. What hope did they have of enjoying motherhood? Some had husbands who already had children and did not care what these young women were going through. Makandida, one of the girls who had a stillborn child in my clinic, was rejected by the husband and was never allowed to go back to him. She was accused of all sorts of things, including witchcraft and possession by demons that fed on babies. After going through this ordeal Makandida had nothing.

When I tried to explain to Makandida what had happened, she did not understand.

"Where is my baby?" she moaned. "My baby! I want my baby now!"

"Makandida, your baby is dead," I said calmly.

"No, no. It isn't true!" she cried. She was so distressed that I had to give her some of my sleeping medicine. With no baby and no husband I did not know how she was going to cope. Poor Makandida!

It was never dull at the clinic – there was always a bit of drama.

Chapter 11: MANYARA

As I lay there waiting for the first pain to cut through my body, my mind was going in all directions. What a thing to go through! From the start, I had shown resentment to Njaidza, the lady in charge. She was a tough woman, very cold and hard-hearted. No, worse – she was heartless. No wonder she didn't have kids. I dreaded to think what kind of mother she would have been, or whether she would have had the courage to cut off her own child's clitoris.

When I tried to run away, the women were prepared. They knew there were always going to be renegades like me. Eventually they caught up with me. I struggled so much that I had to be tied down, with two women holding my legs down. I kicked one in the eye, which made them even more vicious. Days later I still hurt where they had tied me.

The pain of the circumcision – which was done without anaesthesia – was unlike anything I had ever felt in my life. You had to have had this done to you in order to understand the pain I am talking about. I lost a lot of blood, and thought I would never have the strength to walk again.

After the cutting was done I was wrapped with cloths and left to lie down in the temporary shelter where we slept. I was unconscious for a while and all I remember was waking up the following day and seeing other girls lying beside me. I wondered what the women had done with all the bits and pieces they cut off us, but nobody seemed to know or care.

''Why do you want to know so much?'' one of the girls asked. ''Does it matter what they did with the pieces?''

"It's all over and done with anyway," another added. The girls were in too much pain to ask questions like that. After all, what difference did it make? It was only curious Manyara who wanted to know everything.

When I looked at myself that morning I was a wreck. I felt the pain and wetness between my legs and knew that I was still bleeding. I was praying that I would not have problems like other girls I had heard about. I had no control over the result of my circumcision, and only knew I would have scars for life but not how much scarred.

I knew that some problems were inevitable, that girls sometimes even died as a result of the initiation ceremony. Of the girls in my group, none of us were doing well. Some girls were still urinating on themselves because they could not walk, and some screamed with pain as the urine touched the raw skin.

I was quiet. I was trying to harden myself to the pain, and I was busy thinking about my future. *What was so great about this procedure that my mother had been talking about?* I thought to myself. I knew it was evil, and now that it was over, I hated my parents for putting me through it, and I hated everyone who kept this custom alive. How dare they? It was too late for me, what's done was done, but I vowed that day that no child of mine was going to go through that hell, no matter what my mother said.

"One day you will thank me for doing this to you," Njaidza had said. Thank her? How could I? I thought for a minute the old cow had lost it.

Slowly the bleeding started to ease, and I felt thirsty all the time. I had lost a lot of blood, but I was doing better than the rest of the girls. Some of them were being sick and getting more and more weak. Some were still crying for their mothers because of the searing pain.

We were all between the ages of twelve and fifteen – babies who had not known what was in store for us. The idea of leaving our families had felt like a trip to Europe. For most of us, it was the first time we had been away from home, so it had been exciting. The shock of what had happened to us left us all drained.

By late afternoon of the second day, some of the girls were still weak. One girl, Lucia, was still bleeding, and it did not look right. I thought it would be better to let someone know what I was witnessing. We were all told to keep quiet and not share whatever happened at the circumcision with anybody. This was too much to bear. I dragged myself away from the rest of the girls and sat under a tree to write to Maki.

Dearest Maki,

How are you, Maki? I hope you are well. We all have been mutilated, and Maki, I am scared. Lucia is very ill. I think she will die. Some of the other girls are poorly too. I am one of the lucky ones, but I will still have scars for life. Oh, Maki, how can we stop this custom? I am scared, and whatever happens here is hushed up. What are we going to do, Maki?

I hope you get this letter. I don't know when we will be allowed to go back to civilization.

Take care, Maki.

Your friend,

Manyara

I kept my letter for when I went back to the village, but I was happy I had written it. It made me feel better.

I was hoping that none of us would get an infection. I had heard my mother mention this to my father's second wife. That is when I hatched my plan –to try and run away. All of a sudden I was transported back to my stepmother's conversation,

"Worrying, isn't it?" she had said. "You never know what will happen until they are through with it.

"Njaidza is good, though, don't you think?" my father's second wife had asked. "You will not get anyone better in this village. Imagine if mothers were expected to circumcise their kids! I would not be able to do it, would you? I would rather have her than use some of the modern nurses and doctors who seem to know it all."

"It is our way and we cannot do anything about it," my mother had said, "but I worry about infections. Some people have not been able to have kids after their circumcision."

"Maybe they had impotent husbands," my father's third wife had chimed in. "Who knows? I had my circumcision and never had any problems except a bit of itching, which I guess happens with all scars."

"Let's hope all goes well for the girls," my mother had said. "No scars, no clitoral cysts, infections or anything bad. It would be a family curse if they were to have problems."

A girl's scream jolted me back to the present. Njaidza still had some more girls to cut. I was horrified to see a girl of my age being forcefully brought over to the circumcision. She was tied up, just as I had been. She was from the squatters' camp. I did not talk to her at school that much, but I knew that her name was Makandida. Her parents were dead and she was being raised by an uncle. The uncle wanted to get rid of her as soon as he could, so he decided that at twelve she was old enough to be married. All he really wanted to do was make some money out of the marriage.

Makandida, like most girls at my school, was a hard worker. In the morning, before going to school, she went to help in the field. After school she did the same, as well as household chores like fetching water. She would then prepare the food for the family. She was so tired that she used to fall asleep in class. While some of us played in the playground during tea or lunch break, Makandida was always by herself. She was a depressed child, and a thinker. She rarely laughed. I had never seen such a miserable girl.

Being circumcised was not something Makandida wanted – the decision was made by her aunt and uncle. They had already found a husband for her, and because he was an older man it was feared that he might not be able to match her sex drive. Circumcising her would bring a balance. Furthermore, because she was depressed, she was also nervous, and they believed the circumcision would get rid of this. So after the circumcision she would be ready to be taken to her husband.

It was a pity that I could not help the poor girl. I had problems of my own, but at least I had parents to go home to, and no promised husband waiting for me. What a shame that one cannot choose their family. Makandida had no say over her fate.

I thought I should let Maki know of the plight of this unfortunate girl. She might have some suggestions. I don't think Maki knew what kind of woman Njaidza was. So when we got back to the village ,I decided to write to Maki.I knew G would pick up these letters to and fro and it was working for us.

> Dear Maki,
> Things are not good here. I am feeling much better, but I am worried about Lucia. She is not doing well at all and might die from loss of blood. Makandida is being married off after our circumcision. It's a shame that there is no one to speak or fight for her. I wish there was something we could do. Any suggestions, Maki? Don't suggest running away, because she has no relatives other than the wicked aunt and uncle who are marrying her off. Oh, Maki, it's a terrible business. I hope she will be all right.
> Your friend,
> Manyara

And so I was expecting an immediate response, which I got when G got back to the village from the city.

> Dear Manyara,

I thought I should let you know that I will make sure Makandida gets the contraceptive pills as soon as I can get them to her. At least she will be all right. I have read a lot about these women things since my plight. In a few more years she will be able to have children if that's what she wants. Hopefully she will find them useful.

Manyara, I wish I could do more, but for now I really can't come to the village. Keep well, and I know we girls should look after one another.

I miss you.
Your friend,
Maki

A Lost Youth

Chapter 12: NJAIDZA

They say that culture is what makes a people, and that there are no people without a culture. Cultural practices might seem to strange to outsiders, but there is always an explanation for why people believe what they believe as a group. This is what I was thinking as I watched my next group of initiates arriving.

We had them for weeks, to train them and teach them how to be proper women. Circumcision is part of our culture, the culture of our forefathers, and when I am given the opportunity to do my job with these girls I am happy. This practice is part of our cultural identity and helps keep us together as a people. I am happy to take them out of the misery of childishness into womanhood. How can they be women without circumcision? How can they take on the adult responsibility of childbearing? The clitoris and female genitalia are ugly and dirty, and capable of growing to unsightly proportions. This results in making women unclean. This is what people do not understand. This is who we are, and we have to pass it on to the generations to come. Why would we want to hurt our children, our very future? Our children are our future. It is what we impart to them that will allow our culture to survive all the changes of today.

There, I have said it.

A Lost Youth

Chapter 13: MAKANDIDA

My parents had been good people. They were loved by everyone in the village. My mother died from cancer and my father followed a few months later. He seemed unable to survive without my mother. Ranga and I had to be looked after by relations. The moment my aunt on my mother's side said I was to go and live with my uncle, I knew I was in trouble. The Machochos had never been on good terms with my parents. My brother and I were separated, with my brother Ranga staying with my aunt Anna while I went to live with Uncle Machocho and his family. We had never been close, even before the death of my parents, but they were the only relations who were able to take me in.

I knew very well that life would never be the same. I was just nine years old, but I became more of a slave to my uncle and aunt than a child to look after. I had to work for the food I was eating and the fees they were paying for me. Uncle Machocho was ruthless, and as soon as I joined his family he wanted me to give up school. His wife had insisted that I should go for three more years, otherwise people would talk.

Machocho was so impatient that by the time I was eleven, before the three years were up, he had found me a husband and arrangements were made for me to be married off the following year. They received the bride price, and from then on my uncle was stalked me to in case I decided to run away or even sleep with some boy. Even if I had wanted to run away, I had nowhere to go. Besides, I didn't want to lose sight of Ranga. He was happy where he was. Ranga also worked hard, but at least he was going to school. At first he wrote to me until my uncle stopped all communication between us.

The last letter he wrote was so emotional.

Dear Sis,

How are you doing, Makandida? I hope all is well, considering where you are. I hope Mum and Dad are looking after us up there. I miss them, sis, and sometimes I dream of them, talk to them and even laugh with them.

Well, I will look after you, sis. I know I have a better chance of finishing school than you have.

I will pray for us, Makandida. All will be well.

I miss you very much. Bye for now
Your little brother,
Ranga

I cried after reading the letter and since then I have read it so many times. I remember the last one I wrote to him.

Dear Ranga,

How are you doing, brother? I hope all is well your side. It might be a long time before I get in touch again. Don't worry about me, OK? We will be all right. Mum and Dad are looking after us, so we will be all right. How is it with you and Aunt Anna? I know she is looking after you all right.

Oh, Ranga, I miss you so much.

Will be thinking of you always. Take care, my dear.

Your sister,

Makandida

Sometimes I wished I had died along with my parents. Marriage! How could I get married at twelve? My parents had been so set on protecting me against the village custom of men marrying young girls. There was no one to protect me now, and my uncle seemed set on triumphing over my dead parents by making me suffer.

When I first heard about the marriage, I cried my eyes out, but what was I to do? As if that was not bad enough, I was to be taken for the female circumcision- something my parents never believed in. My mother used to spit on parents who took their children for circumcision – and now here I was about to have it done to me. I knew that no one cared about anything I said, so after a few complaints I just gave up. I had no voice as far as my uncle was concerned. I knew I couldn't avoid whatever was coming my way, and I decided to look for a way out once I was old enough.

So I was dragged to the initiation woman, screaming all the way. I guess I hoped someone would see and stop me from being butchered, but I was not lucky. The women held me and tied me down as if I was a sacrificial lamb. I kept screaming, but I felt weaker and weaker, and I started losing blood with the first cut. Before I knew it, they had done it. I had been blindfolded and all I could hear were people pulling my legs apart. My clitoris was cut off and to me that was a crime committed but with no prosecutor or jury to listen. My life will never be the same.

I did not try to ignore the pain. I wanted it to feel it and die. I was praying that I would die in the process – that would have served my uncle right. Unfortunately it didn't happen. I was to live, and forever live in shame.

What happened after the circumcision was like a nightmare. I just kept bleeding, more blood than I had ever seen before. I was weak and drifted in and out of consciousness. Meanwhile my uncle wanted me to come back as soon as I could because my husband was waiting. The idea of losing me was not appealing to him. He could not imagine paying back the money he had taken for my bride price.

Njaidza, the evil woman who did the cutting, insisted I stay until I was healed. My uncle said I had better heal quickly, or he would come there himself to take me home. But how could I go anywhere? I was in so much pain. Eventually the bleeding stopped, but I was still in pain.

I was not allowed to heal properly. My uncle had promised the old man I was married to I would be ready. The moment I returned to the village I was washed, a bag was packed, and I was taken over to the man's house.

"You better behave yourself," Uncle Machocho warned me. "Don't even think of running away. If you do I will catch up with you and beat the hell out of you."

I thought that maybe with a place of my own, life would be a little easier for me and I would be able to do things my way at last. Instead, things got worse. From the moment I got to his house my husband – who, old as he was, had not been married before – expected me to perform full womanly duties. I was to cook and do all the daily household chores. I felt like a slave. And he wanted children. This became an issue in our relationship from the outset; we always argued about it.

The moment I got to his place, he wanted to start having sex. I was only twelve and I was still recovering from mutilation, as Immaculate called it. The first time it happened I thought I was being sliced in half starting with my genitalia. When I started bleeding as well, the sex demands stopped. My husband realized I had to heal, but he was not patient. After a week or so he said we had to have sex again.

"Do you think I don't know your little games?" he said to me. "Excuse after excuse just so you don't get pregnant. I will kill you if you don't give me a child." I had no way of convincing him the wounds were so deep I needed years or maybe a lifetime to heal.

I hurt both physically and mentally, and I had no one to tell. I was miserable and threw myself into work. My old husband had a hut made of poles and mud, with a thatched roof over the kitchen. The bedroom was two rooms made of the same material as the kitchen, but with a tin roof. The bedroom was very sparsely furnished – there was no bed, just a thick mat and a few cheap, itchy blankets. I did not like the smell of the room, so I cleaned it twice a day. I kept the mat out in the sun, which made the old man angry as he thought this would wear out the mat. In the corner of the bedroom there were some old suitcases where we kept our clothes, and an old rickety chair. I used to sit there rocking myself to relax whenever I was upset.

I kept my clothes in my bag as if I was ready to run away, which annoyed my husband. This was my home as far as he was concerned. I still had my doubts. I always thought one day I would get a chance to run away. Without that hope I think I would have committed suicide. My husband did not care how I felt.

Because there was no one to talk to I had to write letters. The first one was to my dead mother.

Dear Mother,

I don't know where to start, but I wanted you to know wherever you are that I wish so much that you were here to look after Ranga and me. Aunt Machocho had me circumcised and now I have a husband. What will they do to me next? Oh, dear Mama, why did you have to leave? I really don't know how I will get out of this. I wanted to go to school like we always discussed. I wanted to be a doctor, but what are my chances now? Oh, dear Mama.

I really hope things will resolve themselves or else I will kill myself.

I will let you know more soon.

Your daughter,

Makandida

I knew that writing to my mother was not going to bring any answers, but it felt better to let it out.

My husband became obsessed with the idea of having children, and the letter I wrote to Maki was really a cry for help.

Dear Maki,

Thanks, Maki, for the contraceptive pills. I will use them with care, because if I am caught there will be trouble. I am not ready and I really want out of this relationship. Life is hard for me now.

Please do help me, Maki. I have also written to my dearest mama.

Your friend,

Makandida

Maki was my only hope as far as this baby talk was concerned. I had no intention of having a baby if I could help it. Each time when I thought I was getting better he would demand more sex and the pain would start again. I never expected this to be an everyday thing. And the pain wasn't just during sex. I always felt pain when urinating and, worse still, struggled with defecating. When was this going to end? I imagined this was my curse for life. I could not go to a hospital – I was too ashamed. What would I say, that my husband is making me sleep with him? Besides, my husband didn't let me out of his sight. He accompanied me everywhere, and I could not even talk to people without him eavesdropping. He did not want me falling in love with a younger man. I felt like a prisoner.

A Lost Youth

Chapter 14: IMMACULATE

I had been enjoying myself pretending all was when finally word came from G. I was to come home. Home, with G and his family. I was scared. As usual, Meju was around – she would be preparing me and taking me to my husband's place.

"They will take you to the city Maki. There is no way I will let G have you live in the same house with his first wife. Very soon you will be a city girl. I told you this was the best way for you. You will be grateful", Meju said excitedly. At this point nothing mattered. I just didn't want to be given to a man –rich or poor.

I had been to the mansion as a visitor, but going there to live was scary. I knew it would be a life-changing ordeal. I was from a different class, and I was going to have two stepchildren. At twelve, who would be mature enough to know what to do with children? I wasn't sure how I was supposed to behave in a house full of servants, either. Even eating was a challenge. Back home I ate from the same plates as my brothers. We did not have to sit at a table, and we enjoyed talking and laughing loudly while we ate. In the short time I had spent in G's house I had realized how differently things were done there.

Although we were poor, the so called- birthday which was in fact a marriage ceremony in disguise had been rich in many ways. To the outside world ,it was a birthday party and I was dying to scream to everyone around that it was a marriage party. There was a lot of food as well as flagons of home-made beer, wines and even some champagne. G had provided for all this. If anyone said they went home empty-handed after the party, they were lying. People were happy. The party was hard for me to take in. It was the explanation given that it was my birthday that made me angry because I knew we never celebrated birthdays. G was around, but he did not come anywhere near me. He was happy, and Meju made sure he was well looked after.

"We should let him see that we will be able to look after him," she said. I tried not to look at him, but I didn't succeed. He was good-looking, but I felt only distaste. I was angry with him. I was angry with everybody. It was a shame I could not cry any longer. I had been crying for a long time, but I had long since realized it was not going to do me any good.

I had enjoyed the time I had with my friends, pretending everything was all right. I had all the fun I could have and my mother let me enjoy being with other twelve-year-olds. All the time I kept hoping the marriage would be called off, but it was too late.

G had always been a mysterious man. Even my parents did not know much about him. I wondered how this arrangement had come to be. Had he approached my parents, or had they approached him? We belonged to different worlds, and I couldn't imagine how my father had got to meet and talk to G.

It was interesting to see my father trying to look and behave sophisticated after the deal had been made with G. He looked much smarter than he had before, and he demanded good food. My mother always rolled her eyes at this. My father used to smoke cheap tobacco, but he now had proper cigarettes thanks to G. He changed so much that it was as if we had a different father.

For my father this marriage was heaven, but sadly for me it was hell. I contemplated killing myself, but then I thought of my mother. And I did not really want to die. My mother was with me through all this and wanted me to be brave.

The day of the party I was dressed in white, like a young bride. My dress was not really a wedding dress, just a white party dress for a twelve-year-old. I was wearing white shoes and socks. Meju had done a good job with my hair. It was neatly plaited with red and white ribbons in it. I was a pretty sight- if only that reflected my whole life, it would have been nice. A couple of days before the party G had one day come over and taken me and Meju to the city. We slept at his house in the city and were taken shopping the next day. I had no experience of shopping. Most of my clothes had been handed down to me by relatives and friends. A couple had been made by local tailors and were just plain, simple dresses. But now G said to me, "Choose what you want, Immaculate, don't be shy."

"Our *Mukwasha* is very generous," Meju said happily. She enjoyed being spoiled. But I was not enjoying this. I knew that in a couple of days my freedom would be at an end.

Meju wanted to take the opportunity to buy me underwear. I did not have much in that area.

I started crying. I wanted to go home.

"Stop being a crybaby, Maki. You do not want G to see you crying, so stop it now. You will soon be a woman."

The more she said that, the more I wanted to holler. "A woman?" I retorted. "What do you mean, a woman?"

"Don't stress yourself now," Meju replied, trying to soothe me. "We don't want you going to your party looking like an unfed street person. Come on now, be a good girl and listen to your aunt."

By the time we got back to G's house I was so upset I went straight to the room where I was sleeping. I locked myself in and refused to open the door, even for G. I did not eat that night, and I cried myself to sleep. The room was well furnished, but the comfort of the room did not ease what was going on in my mind. The big peacock clock could not tell a time when things would be rosy and back to normal for me again. The nice sweet smell in the room did not complement my thoughts. The lights reminded me of the bright life I had dreamt of when I was ten, which now seemed like the distant past. I was doomed. I closed my eyes with nothing but fear in my head. I eventually fell asleep, only to have nightmares.

Meju was very angry with me the next day. When she came to wake me up I did not open the door. I sat in the room thinking. Was I really getting married? What was going to happen to all those dreams I had told my grandfather about? I knew that my grandfather was long dead, but I thought I should write a letter to him, wherever he was. He would understand.

Dear Grandpa,

I don't know where to start, Grandpa. A lot has happened to me since you have left us. I am going to have a husband now instead of a degree from Cambridge or Oxford. What would you do, Grandpa? Did you know my father was planning this? Of all things, why, Grandpa? I know you would not have let this happen if you were alive. I miss you so much and I wish you were here. Remember our stories? My husband-to-be has a big library, but that is no consolation for having to get married.

I don't know what I will do with my life. One thing for certain, I won't kill myself – but I am angry with my parents.

I will write again, Grandfather. Soon. I hope you don't mind. I will let you know if I am allowed to go to school.

Bye for now, Sekuru.

Yours,

Immaculate

I felt better after writing to Grandfather. It felt like talking to God, and I thought things were going to turn out well. The fact that my mother had mentioned the possibility of school kept me going. If it was true, I would have to trust G. I did not know anything about him except all the evil things people talked about. At some point I would have to talk, laugh and even sleep with the devil.

When I finally came out of the room G was waiting by my door with a worried look on his face.

"Are you all right, Immaculate?" he asked. "You had me worried. You need to eat something, then you and I can have a chat." He looked over at Aunt Meju. It was still early, and G was still in his pyjamas. He looked majestic, like a Greek god I had seen in one of the books I had taken from his library. According to Meju, at least I would have good-looking children.

G went to his room and clicked the door shut. What were we going to talk about? I wondered. I tried to imagine the kind of conversation we were likely to have:

"You are my wife now, Immaculate, and you will do as I tell you," he would say.

"You do not own me," I would reply, "and I can do what I want whether you like it or not."

"Don't forget that I paid your parents for you," he would remind me, "so you'd better start behaving."

"You evil man," I would counter, "why don't you go after mature women?"

"I am going to sleep with you tonight," he would tell me.

"You dirty paedophile!" I would scream and run out of the room.

That is how I thought the conversation would go.

Meju interrupted my thoughts. "That was a drama you put on there last night, Maki," she said. "Why? This man is not your enemy, so start behaving like a normal human being before you shame us all. Am I making myself clear?"

"Yes, Meju," I said grudgingly.

"Now go and clean yourself," she told me. "G would like to have a chat."

"Do you know what it is about?" I managed to ask.

"No. Just do as you are told, child, all right?" Meju said.

I could feel the sting of tears in my eyes. I quickly went into the bathroom before I could once again be accused of making a fool of myself by crying. But I needed to cry if I was going to be able to face G. I had to let it out. I had been an obedient child to my parents, but this was beyond what I could take. Whatever he had to say, I had to listen to now.

After my shower, I went to meet him in the study.

"Immaculate, we will talk after breakfast," G told me. "I am not having you starve yourself."

I had been having difficulty eating. My system just refused to cooperate. I was getting thinner and thinner. G and Meju had thought that taking me to the city might help me feel better, but I seemed to be getting worse.

I went to breakfast and forced the food down my throat, but still had to give it back in the bathroom. After that, I went back to G's study. I was both curious and scared of what he was going to say.

Chapter 15: BABA IMMACULATE
(Immaculate's Father)

After Immaculate's marriage, I had a hard time concentrating. Sometimes I talked to myself. At night I had nightmares. I began dreaming of my father. He came to me really angry, and the expression on his face was one of disappointment. He was disappointed with me, but I did what I could for the family. Immaculate had to go to G. We had nearly fought over this. My father, Maki's grandfather had not wanted her to be the sacrificed one. He had suggested we leave it to the next generations but so much was happening. It had to be done.

But I knew I was guilty. I wronged my daughter and would never forgive myself. "I should not have sacrificed my daughter," I said to my wife.

"I told you to leave this alone, and you did not listen," my wife said. "Now Immaculate is gone and it's over. What more can we do now than to hope she will have a fulfilled life? You know as well as I do that this had to be done," she went on. "Maki has to go, and this family will never have peace if she is not married by G. At least she will still be alive."

Who else could have sorted this out? The marriage improved our lives and those of generations to come, but we would never be at peace.

"Culture is what makes us who we are, no matter how complicated it is," I said at the party, thinking out loud. "But what does one do if it gets too complicated? I hate this culture, full of silly rituals and beliefs. My daughter, I cry for my beloved daughter. What does she think of me?"

'Silly man, stop talking yourself into an early grave," my wife said angrily. "What's done is done. Man up. I do not want to be looking after these kids by myself if you die. At least our guests don't know it is a marriage. Let's keep our mouths shut, and I hope you will not forget that in your drunken stupor. It is a birthday party, all right?"

I was a weak man according to my wife. After all, we were husband and wife, and she knew me best.

Chapter 16: G

I did not know what to say about my situation. Nothing was as it seemed. Most people thought I was an old paedophile preying on a young girl. But I was not in that situation because I wanted to be – it was all because of my culture.

I was an educated person and knew right from wrong. I don't know what anyone else would have done in my situation. I was born in a very traditional, old-fashioned family. My family stood by all the old customs and beliefs that were there before I was born. I could not understand this, especially after university. Everything seemed strange.

What would you do if your parents told you a story about your family that you would never understand – a story about an incident that happened years ago, a story about something that happened before you were even born? I tried to convince my family to understand that some of these beliefs were out of step with reality, but they would not hear of it. After all, culture is what makes us, and it has to be passed on for future generations.

"What do you know, you who were born yesterday?" they said to me. Here I was, being made responsible for a situation involving something I did not know about or believe in, something done by my ancestors. How do you explain this to a twelve-year-old girl? Where does one start?

I was dreading the moment I was to meet up with Immaculate again, so innocent and beautiful. The last time I had been close to her was when the traditional ceremony took place seven years ago and I had cried for her. I knew she did not understand a thing at that point because she was too young, but eventually she would grow up and know. Maybe she would hate me for being the chosen husband. I wished that I was not the one involved with this custom.

The moment I was informed of the marriage back then I was upset. I needed time to think. I went away, but when I came back the situation was still waiting for me.

"Don't worry, G, we will wait for you," my great-uncle Rob said. "Take your time. But this has to be done."

I had tried to talk sense to the remaining old relatives, but I was the chosen one. Here is the story of my life.

It is said that my great-grandfather, Munarwo, left home when he was a young boy to look for employment. He walked for days and days, then was taken in by another family. They gave him food and asked him if he wanted to work for them. Munarwo accepted the job offer, which included herding cattle and working on the farm. He was a lovely boy, and the family liked him.

Then something happened. Munarwo fell in love with Evernice, the daughter of the family. They accepted the relationship, but even poor as he was, Munarwo was expected to pay a bride price. Of course he could not, so it was agreed that he would work for ten years for the bride price; only then would he get his wife.

Ten years was a long time, but Munarwo loved his fiancée and agreed to wait. He saw each day as part of his quest to be with Evernice. They were both happy with the arrangement, and knew that in the end they would be together forever. They were not to share a room or have sexual relations until the bride price was paid. This was no problem, since they were both young.

Years went by, and there was an outbreak of malaria; Munarwo became sick. They tried every medicine they could, but sadly Munarwo did not survive.

The family was devastated, and so was Evernice. By this time, Munarwo had worked for more than half his bride price, and according to custom, he was married to Evernice. She vowed to stay single for the rest of her life.

But Evernice fell in love again. According to the tradition of those days, Evernice had been as good as married and needed special traditional cleansing in order to be another man's wife. The spirit of the dead man needed to be separated from her. If this was not done, it was said that the family and all the generations to come would pay dearly by being cursed with something called *ngozi*. Evernice had to be free of the dead man's spirit. In my world this does not make sense, but this is the story that has made me who I am today.

In order for the cleansing to be done, Evernice and her family had to find Munarwo's family and negotiate with them. But no one knew where he came from, and Evernice's parents' efforts to find his family were unsuccessful. In the end no cleansing was done.

Evernice got married anyway, and life seemed normal. There were no mishaps or anything out of the ordinary. *Ngozi,* however, does not affect the immediate generation. It always waits and resurfaces only after the older generation has all gone. So my great-grandfather's and grandfather's generations were not affected.

But my father felt that something had to be done to protect all our lives, including my wife's, forever. Because we were the wronged ones, we had to be compensated. We had to get the bride, and I was the chosen groom. Immaculate's family is said to have consulted everyone they could from prophets to spirit mediums until they found my family. Coincidentally we had ended up in the same area- the very reason my family believed it was meant to happen. We were guided by the dead man's spirit so it had to be done.

Chapter 17: MARIA

At first becoming G's wife was the best thing that ever happened to me despite the complications. At first I wasn't sure that he was going to marry; he seemed to be a wanderer. When he went to study abroad, I honoured him by waiting. It wasn't easy – I was under a lot of pressure from friends and relatives to forget about G and go for men who were available, men who were organized and serious about life. And besides, there was always gossip when we were dating about him having to marry a *ngozi* wife. But I wanted G. He was kind man. I knew there must be a reason he did not want to settle down. I knew about the *ngozi* that had nearly sent him to a seminary, but in the end he told me the whole truth. I knew he was going to be given a young girl but I didn't know he was going to fall in love

It was when he came back from East Germany.

''Maria, I am afraid I have some bad news for you,'' he said. "I know I should have told you before, but this is it, you have to know."

I laughed, but G was not laughing. *It must be serious, then*, I thought to myself.

"I am afraid we can't get married," G said.

I was fuming. ''How dare you!'' I said. I had waited for him, and now this! ''Who do you think you are?'' I said angrily.

G explained his situation, and in the end I understood. But at that point the family in question had no girl child. So we had to wait for a girl to be born. I hoped that no girl would be born out of that family so that G could be mine, but unfortunately Immaculate came along.

My husband was troubled by all this, and I could have taken him away, but there was no chance. Reluctant as he was, he had to rescue his family. I felt for him. So I went straight into this marriage knowing that there would be another wife and I would have to live with it.

When the traditional ceremony was done when the girl – Immaculate – was five, I knew it was finally happening and I had to accept it. The problem was, my poor husband was so generous. What could he not do for Immaculate's family? Sometimes I worried that we would be left bankrupt. But I knew I had to stand by him.

I knew that people talked and accused him of all kinds of evil things, but he did nothing wrong. Oh, my poor husband!

Chapter 18: IMMACULATE

I did not know what was in store for me when G said he wanted a word. A word with G only meant one thing as far as I was concerned, being stopped from going to school. I was prepared to howl in his room.

When I knocked on his door he was ready and waiting. But when I went into his bedroom, he had his back to me. I knew things were not right.

"Immaculate, we need to talk," he said. "I know you want to go to school, but it will have to be a school away from home and you would be all by yourself. Will you be all right? Do you still want to go?" He paused. "I wanted to tell you a story about you and me," he said, "but I guess it's too early. We will leave it for now and talk about school. What do you think we should do?"

I did not know what to say. G was offering me the chance to go on with school. Could I believe him?

"Don't you think we should talk to Meju about this?" I asked.

"Oh, forget Meju," he said. "This is between you and me and what *we* want." He winked at me.

Despite his lightheartedness, I was still scared of G. Nothing had changed between us. He was my enemy, and no chit-chat was going to change that. But for now I was stuck with him.

I knew my friend Makandida was also married at twelve, and that she never had any peace. The letters from her were worrying. I was on the verge of mental stress myself, but thinking about Makandida writing to her dead mother was even more upsetting. At least both my parents were alive.

I could not imagine what was going in Makandida's mind at this point. She had gone through the most awful ordeal – female genital mutilation – and was in an abusive relationship. What more did a young girl have to go through? I had to try to help her, and I thought I could get some birth control pills from a friend who was a nurse. It was the most difficult thing for me to do because I felt like a harlot. These pills were not sold over the counter and to get many would have required help. To make it worse ,I would be considered too young to purchase such pills.

"Georgina, could you please get me some contraceptive pills?" I asked my friend.

"Immaculate, what do you want them for? I didn't think you and G were actually having sex or are you?" Georgina asked.

"For a dear friend, Georgina, not for me," I assured her. "G and I , heavens no! Can you help me, please?"

I had explained to Georgina why I was in need of such a large amount of contraceptive pills and the risks my friend would be taking if her husband caught her with these pills. In the end she gave me a big bag of pills. I did not ask how she got them, but I was grateful. I had to make sure they were passed over to the village for Makandida. Makandida's husband kept demanding sex, even when she was in pain from the genital mutilation.

I was lucky that I hadn't gone through this procedure. My family always thought female genital mutilation was a heinous crime against women. But they did not object to marrying me off to G.

There must be some explanation, though, I always thought.

....
....

As I sat in his bedroom with him, G was calm. He knew I was always tense around him, so he tried to put me at ease.

"Do you think you will be happy living with us, Immaculate?" he asked me.

"I don't know, G," I replied. "I never dreamed I would be married at twelve. Do you really need another wife?"

G could only laugh, but it was not a happy laugh. He was as stressed by the whole situation as I was.

"I don't need another wife, Immaculate," he told me, "but this is the situation we are in and we have to cope somehow."

"What situation is that, G?" I asked.

"There is more to the story between us, Immaculate," he said. "I guess neither Meju nor your parents have told you the full story."

I was curious, but G would not tell me any more.

I was fascinated by his room and as I looked around, I forgot for a while what we were talking about. The room was large and beautifully furnished – I loved it. It was very spacious, and I was spellbound by the number of books that were there.

"You have so many books", I commented unnecessarily.

After a few moments, G began to talk again. "The truth is, Immaculate," he said, "you and I are victims of our culture."

"What do you mean?" I asked.

At that moment Meju knocked on the door. She wanted to know if I was behaving.

"She is doing well, Meju," G assured her. "Don't worry," he added, with obvious irritation, "I will handle her. Maybe Immaculate and I will have to finish our conversation later."

"No, no, go on," Meju said quickly. "I will sit in the other room."

This was the first time I understood G's attitude towards Meju. His patience with her was running out. So was mine, I guess. Meju, always inquisitive. Now that she had done her job, she behaved as if she owned me. If there was a time when I wanted her help, it was long gone. I had wanted her to use her power to stop my parents from marrying me off. She had failed me, and to me she was now a useless aunt.

....
....

Although it did not change my situation, my chat with G was fruitful in many ways. It was nice to get to know him on a personal level. Tough as he seemed to the villagers, he was the softest man I had ever known. He was kind and genuine in his conversations with me. We were both angry, but being angry at each other was not going to help. We decided early on to be civil and friendly to one another, and act as if we were all right. This worked, at least for a while.

One thing I gathered from my conversation with G was that we were not going to have a sexual relationship at all, which I was happy with at first. I was not sure, though, whether he was giving me the chance to mature first or whether it was a change in our terms and conditions.

The thing I liked most was that I was free to go to school. Anything else did not matter at this point as far as I was concerned. The problem was deciding where I was to go to school. Obviously people would talk if I was to live with G's family in the village. He could not let me live in one of his houses in the city, as I was too young. So it had to be a boarding school. I was happy to go anywhere.

Meju was not happy about it, though. She thought G was giving me too long a rope, which I might hang myself with. According to her, I should stay at home and have children. It was not until later that I understood why she was so worried. I was not to be trusted in case a younger man might tempt me into his bed and jeopardize everything.

But the decision was made. Immaculate was going to school. We spent a few more days with G, and then we headed back to the village.

I was married, but I was happier than my friends who were in similar situations. I would be starting school soon and the prospect of a boarding school was exciting. Not many people in the village knew about boarding schools. There were good schools run by different missions, and most of the schools for girls were run by Catholic nuns. Meju had suggested I go to such a school. It was all fun for me, and I didn't care which school I went to. All I wanted was a normal life.

Chapter 19: IMMACULATE

When I was thirteen I got a place at a school run by nuns. It was one of the best Catholic schools in the country, Nagle House. Founded by the Presentation Sisters from Ireland, inspired by Nano Nagle, this was a perfect school for me. Pupils came from all over the country and no one would know or ask questions about G or my family.

The school was amazing. Built in the quiet suburb of Marondera, surrounded by tall willow and gum trees, it felt like heaven. The yard was peaceful and neatly maintained, filled with well-looked-after plants. From the front you could see the reception, and at the back was the massive chapel, which was used as a hall when the whole school gathered for special occasions. There was the common room, the dining hall and our precious big library. I fell in love with the place immediately. I was shown to my room and fell in love with my roommate, Jess. Things were turning out to be better than I had expected. *How will I ever be able to thank G?* I thought to myself.

Nobody here knew about my marriage. G looked like just another parent or guardian dropping his kid off at school.

My parents and G promised to visit, and after waving everybody goodbye, I settled in to get ready for the journey ahead. I was so grateful for the opportunity I was given to go to one of the best schools. In fact, things were going so well that I started to get worried. It was too perfect; I thought my happiness might be snatched away.

Despite all this good fortune, there was still some mysteriousness around the whole marriage business, and I wasn't sure what to make of it now that I was here.

That year I had my first period, and I got really scared. I had been reading a lot about reproduction and I knew I could now get pregnant if I was to engage in unprotected sex. I did not tell anybody, not even my friends at school, who envied me because they thought I had more than everyone else. At thirteen I knew that now if I slept with a man without protection I would become pregnant.

G visited frequently, and that's when I got embarrassed with my friends. I couldn't tell people he was my father, but at the same time I couldn't say he was my husband. I was worried he might do things that would make people suspect that he was my husband, but he didn't. All I got was a hug and a peck on the cheek. G would bring food and give me pocket money, and he made sure I had all the books I needed. The other girls thought I had a rich uncle who was taking care of my welfare. I felt spoiled. On Fridays I enjoyed going shopping in town with other girls. It felt like one of those things I used to read about in books. I never dreamt I would be able to enjoy life so much after being handed over to G.

I continued to work hard because I really thought I ought to keep G happy. Every holiday I had to go to G's house in the city before visiting my parents in the village. Most of the time I chose to spend my school holidays in the city. I was different but I was happy. Back home in the village, people said that G had transformed me into an alien. When would I learn how to work in the fields, fetch water and do the other chores women did?

My marriage was still being kept secret but my guess was people knew. All people were told was that my fees were being paid by a Good Samaritan. My family were happy for me.

Although I had been uprooted from the village I still had friends there. Norest was still one of my best friends, but Meju insisted on ending the friendship now that I was married. I still gave him books, though. Makandida, Manyara and Egifa kept in touch by writing letters from time to time, updating me on what was going on in the lives of my classmates from the village. I also wrote to them.

Dear Manyara,

How are you doing, guys? I just wanted to check on you. I am happy going to school. The school is nice, and G is looking after me – but not in the sexual way. How about you, Manyara? How is Norest doing? Is he still doing well in class? Does he have a girlfriend? Give him my regards.

I am still doing well in school. I will tell you all about it next time.

See you soon.

Your friend,

Immaculate

G always brought me letters from my village friends. I was sad when I heard that some had dropped out of school.

G also wrote to me, but none of his letters were in any sense romantic. They were mainly letters of assurance that everything would be all right. One of the letters I recall was written the week after I had left for boarding school.

Dearest Immaculate,

I hope you are well and I hope school is all right. I know I should not worry, but I miss you, Immaculate.

Have you got enough food? Do write if you need anything, will you, Immaculate? Remember I am here for you.

Keep smiling.

G

At first I didn't want to respond to G's letters, but I felt bad, so in the end I did. I have kept all the letters and I read them with great joy.

Dear G,

Thanks for writing to me. I will admit I feel homesick. I miss my family and friends.

As for food, do not worry, G, I have more than enough. Have to go now – the study bell has just rung.

I will write. Thanks, G, for everything.

Immaculate

Writing to him became a hobby. I came to expect a letter from G every week, and I think he did from me. Whenever I spent a holiday in his house I could see the box of my letters on his desk.

In some of his letters he simply updated me on how well his business was doing. Sometimes it was all about his daughter and her love life. I had nothing to say in that regard.

One evening during a school holiday in my A Level year, I came home late after some time out with friends. When I got in G was waiting for me. I was scared. He had a frown on his face, which made my heart pump like a grinding machine. I quickly tried to escape to my room, but he beckoned me over to where he was standing. I asked him what he wanted.

"You realize you are a married woman?" he asked.

"Yes, G, how can I forget?" I replied.

"Just be careful," he told me. "I don't want trouble."

I knew G found this sort of conversation difficult, but he had to say it. By that time I had grown into a beautiful young woman, and I was never short of admirers. Sometimes men would accompany me home, and G watched this with interest – although, despite everything, he seemed uninterested in me. That was all very well, but I was getting scared of making bigger plans for myself, scared that I might even fall in love.

"Is that all, G?" I asked.

"No, Immaculate," he told me. "Are you busy right now? Do you mind sitting with me for a while? I will have tea brought in so that we can talk."

The word 'talk' scared me. Being called for a talk with G always made me wonder if it was going to be the long-awaited talk about sex. The tea came, and when the maid had gone G asked me what I wanted to do after A Levels.

"University, I guess," I said.

"Good for you," he told me. He looked tired, which made me worried. I had grown very fond of him. He treated me well, and I could not have asked for a better husband. Unlike my friends who had been married off at the same time as me, I was doing well. I had heard that Makandida had a medical condition called obstetric fistula that had led to her husband abandoning her. Manyara was pregnant. Yet here I was, sitting with my husband and talking about university. I was happy to be allowed to plan my future. But I worried about G. He was in his late fifties now and was still looking athletic and handsome, but I sometimes worried about what would happen to me if he was to die – would I be a free woman? I did not want him to die.

"Are you all right, G?" I asked.

"Immaculate, dear, I am all right," he assured me. "Don't strain your pretty face with worry. I am just tired." My heart went out to him. I poured the tea for him and we went on talking.

"Would you consider going abroad for university if you were given the chance?" he asked.

I was shocked. Why was this man being so generous? Was I missing something here? It was not that I didn't want to go abroad – that had been my dream. But at this point it felt as if I was being sent away because he did not want me. I had been preparing myself for the day when I would be expected to perform wifely duties, but suddenly it seemed that that was not going to happen. I felt that I was being rejected.

G was my husband, and I didn't expect him to treat me like a sister for much longer. If men saw me as attractive, surely I must have appealed to G as well – but he never showed any interest in me. I was starting to get worried. It was my last year at school and there were times when I felt lonely. I did not have a boyfriend, and I did not want to have an affair. As I blossomed into a woman I had my moments of wanting a man's cuddle or a kiss. But G never showed any interest.

Meju kept on asking me whether we had "done it." She meant sex.

"For your information, no," I finally told her, "and maybe never will."

"I wonder what this man is playing at," she said, more to herself than to me.

I too began to wonder – what was this marriage really for?

"G, what if I go abroad and don't come back? How is that going to work?" I asked him. "Are you sure that is what you want?"

"If that is what you want, we can talk about it and see what can be done," he said.

"Really?" I asked, worried.

"Immaculate," he said, taking a deep breath, "I think it's time you knew the truth about us."

I looked at him questioningly. "The truth?" I asked.

"Yes," said G. "The truth. I don't think Meju or your father explained to you what this marriage is all about, and you have a right to know. Your family is compensating my family for a tragedy that happened years ago. Your true husband is the spirit of a dead man. I am only his representative. Your family believe they will not prosper until that perturbed spirit is put to rest by being given a wife he paid a bride price for but did not receive generations ago."

What actually happened was after years of searching your family found my family through the mediums and here we are. The marriage would finally go through, generations after the original marriage

G explained to me that his great-grandfather had died before marrying his wife, who was from our family. A lot of bad things had been happening in my family which were associated with this spirit, G's great-grandfather, wanting what belonged to it. G said that my family was upset to have to make me the sacrificial lamb, but there was no other way out. At first they had not known what to do, as everyone in the family kept having only boys. Then, when everyone had given up hope, I was born – a girl at last. I was the chosen one. I was to go and settle this matter so that the next generations would finally have a peaceful life. It had to be done when I was still young, otherwise they knew I would not have gone to G's family.

I was not to be married to another man. I was to carry G's family's name until I died. It was said that if I ever had another man in my life, the spirit would kill him. The only other alternative was for me to carry G's child. That child would be the spirit's child, and that would break the curse. Unfortunately for me, G did not want to take this route. He did not want to think of his child as the dead man's property.

G told me that I was welcome to stay with his family and do whatever I wanted, as long as I remembered that I was a married woman.

By the time G got to the end of this story, I was numb with shock. I got up and started walking around. I did not know what to do. Suddenly I knew that my life was not just as simple as I thought-being married off but it was more than that. How was I to get out of this one? As it sank in – that there was never to be a normal married life for me, that I was married to a ghost for now and for always – I started to scream.

"No, no, no!" I screeched at the top of my voice. "This isn't true!" G reached out to me, but I wanted to be left alone. I ran upstairs and locked myself in my room.

That night I did not sleep. I felt doomed. "*I have to do whatever it takes to get out of this even if it means sleeping with G*", I kept on telling myself. According to this belief, I would never be free of Munarwo's spirit. I would never have a real marriage; I would never have kids who would be free of Munarwo's spirit. How was I to get myself out of this one?

All of a sudden it all made sense – my mother crying all the time, my father avoiding me, and my brothers' sympathy. I was angry with everyone in my life. I needed answers – from G, Meju and my parents.

The next morning I rushed down the corridor to G's bedroom. As I passed one of the big mirrors on the wall, I could not help noticing how puffy my eyes were from crying. My face was so drawn I thought I was seeing a ghost. I didn't care. I knocked insistently at the door. G answered quickly, as if he had been waiting for me.

G looked as if he had been up all night. I fell into his arms, but this time I was not going to cry. I needed to talk. I realized that I had matured overnight. *"Think straight Immaculate, think, don't do something you will regret"*, that voice of reason kept on surfacing. What was the voice of reason- being a dead man's wife? I was angry and at this point didn't care about life and dreams. I was giving up and knew what I was going to do.

G sat me down and started with an apology.

"I am sorry, Immaculate," he said. "I had to tell you because I did not want you ever to hope for a family with me. I already have a family, whom I love. Things between you and me will remain exactly as they are."

"Why did you accept having me as your wife, then?" I wanted to know. "And does your wife Maria know about this? I don't understand any of it, G."

"I am here for you, Immaculate," he assured me, "and I will always be, so don't worry your pretty face." He was trying to make light of the issue, but I would not hear of it.

"So tell me," I said to him, "when was this marriage to a ghost formalized?"

G told me that the party I had when I was twelve was just a modern version of the marriage. I was only five when all the formal traditional procedures were carried out. Traditional beer was brewed, and old men from both sides of the family had evoked the dead man's spirit and let it know I was the wife. I was to bear children for him through G if that's what he wanted. G and I had been made to sit side by side while we were covered by a white cloth. The few people who were invited danced and clapped to the music. From that day on I was married.

G said I had lain as if dead, rolling my eyes, while the ceremony was carried out, and that was a sign that I was communicating with the spirit of the dead man. I was possessed by the spirit for more than half an hour. That meant everything was going to be all right.

I had no recollection of any of it, but I knew G was telling the truth.

"Why did you not refuse?" I asked him.

He told me that he had refused at first, but he had no power against the elders. They knew what was right, and he had to comply. "And it would not have made any difference for you, Immaculate," he added quietly. "Your fate was sealed the day you were born."

I stood by G's bedroom window thinking about my next move again. *Surely there must be a way out for me*, I thought to myself. Could I run away? What was the point, with this cloud always hanging over me? I thought of what G had said about going abroad. I will still go abroad and still have the spirit following me. I also thought about becoming a nun, but I knew I didn't have the belief or commitment for that. I thought about having G in my bed, if that would help break the curse. None of the options was easy since the outcome was not assured. The words from my brother-"whatever you do, the spirit will be following you", did not make life any easier.

G remained seated. We were both exhausted. I had thought about it all night and I had made up my mind: I would have G's child. I would have to go against my principles. What would it matter now? What was the point if I was domed like that? I had to something desperate here- seduce a man who had shown no interest in me whatsoever.

"Can I come and sit by your bed?" I asked.

"Of course you may," said G. "I will be leaving soon. I have a meeting."

I was still wearing my nightdress. I walked across the big room and headed for G's bed. I covered myself with the duvet. If I could sleep with him once, I thought, I might get pregnant and have a baby. I would see to it that my baby was *my* baby, and I would protect him or her from the evils of the world, no matter what it took to do so. That was wishful thinking but I had heard that if I had a baby the spirit would focus on the child and I would be free. But what about my baby?

At that moment, I wasn't thinking that I still had to do my A Levels and that G had never shown any interest in me. I just knew that this was my only chance. I was hoping he would come to bed. I didn't know what it would be like to have a fifty-five-year-old man in my arms. I felt as if I was trying to make an honest man bad. He had been so nice to me and had never asked for anything; here I was, hoping he would do what I had thought all this time he had been dying to do. I touched his arm. There was no going back for me and I think I was now possessed by the dead man's spirit.

"Immaculate," he said gently, "I do not think you know what you are doing now. Don't look for trouble." But that was not going to stop a desperate me.

I knew what I was doing. I saw my dreams coming to nothing. Consummating the marriage was the only way out. I knew I was an attractive, sexy girl and could take advantage of the moment. I got out of bed and took off my nightdress, then stood before G stark naked.

"Immaculate, please cover yourself," he said. How can you do this? I can see the spirit has taken over you body. This is not like you", G added but I was not going to be dissuaded from my mission. Maybe I was possessed.

But I was as ripe as a fresh mango, with rounded breasts, and as his eyes moved towards my womanhood, I could tell like Adam in the garden of Eden he was not going to resist. He had to let go of the tension he'd been holding ever since I was twelve. It had taken us six years to do what was expected of us years ago.

I moved over to him and did exactly what I had gathered from my years of growing up-touched his private parts. He looked aside but he could not resist any longer. Our lips came together as if drawn by a magnet and before I knew it his hands were all over me and we were on the king-sized bed. All the politeness of the past years seemed to disappear with our yearning for each other.

G was a good lover and gentle with me. We explored each other's bodies as if we were meeting for the first time. I enjoyed it.

When we finished we looked at each other and started crying. It was all over now. It was a shock for both of us but the barrier was broken. All of a sudden I felt shy G had vowed to his wife that he was not going to sleep with me, and I had promised the same. But it had happened. I had made love to a married man.

G cancelled his meeting and we spent the whole day in bed. We talked as well.

"Where do we go from here, Immaculate?" G asked.

"Back to where we were before," I said after some time. "We have to stop before it goes further."

"Let's hope we can," he agreed. "Please do not tell anyone. I am to blame. I should not have got carried away."

"Did you see this coming, G?" I asked.

"I am not sure, Immaculate," he replied, "but I feel that the burden I have been carrying is now lighter."

I wasn't sure whether this was going to turn out well or badly. Where was this going to take me? I did not want to start fighting with G's wife, but surely she was not going to let me have G. And I was not sure I was ready for a husband. I was just a repressed seventeen-year-old girl who had been dreaming of having sex. I also thought I was taking control of my situation for once. I didn't think it would really happen between me and G.

I wanted to know more about G. Was it true he had killed children to enhance his riches? Was it true he was educated in the Soviet Union? G laughed when I told him some of the things the villagers had said about him. He had been educated in East Germany and had never been to the Soviet Union. He had made his money through hard work. He had a doctorate in Electrical Engineering and was the co-founder of four companies that dealt with electricity. It was nice to finally know the truth. All what the villagers has said about G was lies.

"What's with the German name?" I asked him. He laughed. He was born Goredema, a name he detested. When he did his Master's degree in East Germany he had changed his name to Goetz, calling himself G for short.

I thought I needed to write to one of my friends and clear all the untrue gossip that had been said of G. This time it was to Egifa. She had been updating me on her progress in Zambia.

Dear Egifa,

How are you doing? I hope you have not forgotten us. School is good and so is my social life. I got intimate with G, can you imagine that? So unexpected, but I enjoyed it. I don't know what we are going to do from now on. Remember my wish to go to Europe. I am still intending to do that though as you might want to know, the dead man's spirit will still follow me. I don't know what to do next though..

What degree are you planning to do? I am thinking of Engineering. That's what G did as well.

Bye for now.

Your friend,

Immaculate

The next few days before I went back to school were great. It felt like heaven. G and I thought that what happened had been a one-off thing, and we were not going to do it again – but we were wrong. It happened again and again. I had changed and I guess the fact that I was a dead man's wife somehow made me careless with life.

We did not talk about our situation again. I still felt guilty about it, and a part of was really hoping I would get pregnant. I kept on suppressing the voice of reason in me that reminded me I was playing careless and could get pregnant and might regret. I was not sure what G's wife would say if I did – maybe a divorce was on the way. I really did not want to see G hurt, but we had done it and there might be consequences.

It was entirely my fault. I had tempted the man. I had been a woman on a mission, and no man would have resisted me at that time. At least the constant lovemaking was helping to distract me. I did not know what the future held for me, and hoped I would manage to get pregnant and break the curse.

On the day I went back to school, we spent half the day in bed exploring each other's bodies and talking about the future. G drove me to school late in the evening and then had to go back and explain talk to his wife in the village.

I was scared. I had to write to Manyara. Six years earlier I didn't think I would be telling my friends this, but I owed it to them. They had always kept me up to date with their issues.

Dearest Manyara,

I thought I would let you know this. I seduced the big man into bed. If you are wondering who, it's G, and if your next question is why – it's because of the story he told me.

I envy all of you in a way, because my story is a shameful one. Ndiri mukadzi wengozi.[12] I guess it's my excuse for seducing him, but I was livid when I found that out. Not one member of my family mentioned any of this to me. Can you imagine? How awful! These people actually fooled me and hid the truth from me. How can I ever trust my family again? Oh, Manyara, I didn't know, but now that I do I am going to enjoy myself. What else can I do? The sex is good, though. It was magical the first time. I won't go into detail now, but I will keep you posted. I know I sound hypocritical, but what choice do I have now? G is looking after me as always, and I am grateful. Now he can't stay away. I am like his princess. I have to keep him away, otherwise I won't pass my A Levels. I know what you are thinking, that I would never fail exams. I know, but you never know. One has to work hard all the time.

What my family has done to me has made me more determined to go abroad. I want to fulfil my dream, no matter what it takes. I promised my grandfather I would study at Cambridge, and G has promised he will make this happen. Maybe he hopes I will stay with him, but Manyara, I am not sure.

Anyway, what started as a short letter is now turning into a very long one.

I miss you, Manyara.

Your friend,

Immaculate

That term I worked harder than I had ever done before. I still did not know what I would do- whether to pursue my dream of going to England or stay around with, so I needed my good grades.

I also realized I had not fallen pregnant, which was fine with me. G was not going to stop making love to me now that we had started. I knew that the more often we had sexual intercourse, the more likely I was to get pregnant and then be free.

---

[12] I am a wife of a dead spirit.

A Lost Youth

The one-off pact we had made when we first made love was long since forgotten. During half-term week he picked me up from school and we went straight to a hotel he had booked for us. We had fun, but I still wanted to know all was well with his wife. G, however, did not want to talk about it. It was our time. Everything had changed.

"So what do you think will happen to me, G?" I asked one afternoon, kissing his nose. "Do you still want me to go abroad?"

"Immaculate, my dearest," he replied, "much as I love you, I would not want to keep you if you really want to go."

Did he say 'love'? I thought to myself. That was the first time he had mentioned the word 'love'. Was he in love with me, then? I had not seen G as a lover, but as my protector and provider. I had hoped he would not fall in love with me. I was getting the good life – the sex and the opportunity to do what I wanted in life – but I had not fallen in love with G. How many people get such an opportunity? So far, so good for me.

Chapter 20: G

I never thought I would do what I did – have sex with Immaculate. I had always seen my self as Immaculate's protector, her liberator – not her lover. All I had seen ever since she was five was a lovely little girl who was a victim of her culture. What happened between us that day came as a surprise. I am sure now Immaculate had been possessed by the spirit of the dead man. I had made a promise to my wife that I would not sleep with her. I should have seen it coming, but I had not expected her to turn into such a pretty young woman, such a temptress.

Of course my wife was angry when she found out, and my world began falling apart. I was worried that people in the city would think I had raped her or used my money to win her. Everything changed. I should have stayed away from her. I had not planned to have sex with a twelve-year-old – nor, for that matter, a twenty-, thirty- or even forty-year-old Immaculate. I wanted what was the best for her – to follow her dream. Then she chose my body. I guess one can not blame her. She felt let down by life and loved ones and wanted to get back something out of that misery. I knew she was playing a part in all this.

I did not know how to deal with the situation. The more I tried to resist her, the more I kept going back to her for more sex, laughter and company. I even found myself sneaking behind my wife's back to be in the city with Immaculate. She no longer wanted to come to the village, even to see her parents. I knew she was trying to hurt them as much as they had hurt her. She wanted to show them that she didn't care, yet deep down she loved them.

I could never bring my wife and Immaculate together. Whose bed would I share – that of my wife, whom I love-much as people had said the contrary, or that of Immaculate, childish yet fun? I felt young when I was with her. Who said an old man cannot do with young blood?

Call me a crazy old man, but I fell in love with her. She was something in bed. I hoped she would agree to share me with my wife and stop talking about going abroad. I wondered if she would agree to marry me if I got a divorce from Maria.

I was ashamed of myself, but I knew I could never stop seeing her. I considered myself an evil man. I should have let her make her own decision about the whole situation. Oh, Immaculate, what did you do to me, darling? The spirit of the dead man seemed to be in control of my body. Never have I felt so crazy over a woman in my life-not even my wife. If I could only have things the way they were before!

Chapter 21: MAKANDIDA

I have never understood men. But maybe if we had met at the same level, I would have tried to understand the man I got stuck with.

He was ruthless. I tried over and over to be good to him, to cook and wash for him, but he was an ungrateful old man. Eventually I started fighting back. I would cook for him, leave the food in the kitchen and then go straight to bed. It only worked for a week. After that he demanded that we eat together and go to bed together. I knew what that meant – he wanted sex.

I wasn't going to let him do anything to hurt me any more. I had been with him for a year by then, and he was getting more and more irritated by the fact that I was not pregnant. The truth is, my old friend Immaculate had sent me a bag full of birth control pills. She had said she would use them if she were me, because it was hard being a baby and having to look after one. In the letter she had sent with the pills she wrote,

"You have to look after yourself Makandida. Use these contraception pills and you will not regret it. No pressure, hon, but have a think about it."

Typical of Immaculate – helping out wherever she can. Thank God she knew so much from all the reading she does-at least now she knows how to help people like me. I was so thankful to her. The moment I realized how abusive my husband was, I decided that the best thing to do was to deny him what he wanted most – children.

I could not possibly keep the pills in the house. I had a place outside for them and sneaked out every day to take one. This worked well for two full years, and the tension between us was high. I was slapped many times, and when we were having sex he would swear and say all sorts of ugly things to hurt me, but I didn't care. I did not want to have a child with this man, so I ignored whatever he said.

Making love was a punishment for me. I did not recover fully from my circumcision, and the wounds never had a chance to heal. He had no respect for me, and when I said sex was painful he would just swear.

I wrote to Maki again. I didn't know how long it took for my letters to reach her, but it felt better to write. G though always brought letters to the village for us from Maki.

Dear Maki,

Thanks for being my friend. At least I get the chance to tell someone how I feel. I did not know sex could be such a painful thing. I hate it when the sun sets because I now know it means hell for me. My body goes on fire. Makato is rough in whatever he does with me and I feel disgusted. I just want him to stop, but how can I get him to do that? Now I understand why some women have been accused of killing their husbands. Makato is cruel and I hate him. I get all the insults you can think of because I am not getting pregnant.

I am happy knowing I won't get pregnant as long as I take those pills. Oh, Maki, thank you so much.

Wish me luck.

Missing you,

Makandida

For me, sex was never enjoyable. All I did was open my legs and start having a conversation in my mind with my imaginary lover. My imaginary lover would say all the nice things and touch me softly, and I would moan with pleasure. In real life, it was my husband who was on top of me, raping me, and I was moaning in pain. Such was my life as a married woman.

On my fourteenth birthday my husband wanted to have a word with my uncle about my situation. If I was barren he wanted his money back.

My aunt had a go at me. What game was I playing at, she wanted to know. Was someone behind this barrenness? She told me that if I didn't get pregnant soon, I would end up on the street.

When we came back my husband was pleased with himself. He could see how shaken I was. As usual, I cooked and we ate together. I did not try to make conversation with him. I always ate in silence, which annoyed him. I had nothing to say.

Then I made a blunder that nearly cost me my life. I sneaked out to my hiding place for the tablets. This time, though, my husband followed me. When he saw what I had in my hand he went berserk. He pulled me by the hair into the house, along with my bag of birth control pills. He hit me everywhere –my face was bleeding and my eyes swelled up.

I started to scream, but he kept saying, "Quiet, you witch. All this time I was wasting my time and you were busy taking this rubbish. Did you think I was not going to catch you?"

He threw the pills in the fire. I crouched down on the floor, covering my face.

"Ungrateful bitch," he barked. "You should be ashamed of yourself."

I thought that was it, but I was mistaken. He took me to my uncle's house and told him what had happened. I was further beaten by my uncle, who demanded to know who had given me the pills. I refused to mention any names, so the beating got worse. By the time we went back home I was unconscious.

My husband threw me into bed. I was in pain, and my eyes would not open, but that night my husband felt it was fair to make me pay for my sins. He made love to me as if he was possessed. He raped me over and over. I was in pain and I silently took it all.

The same pattern continued for the next couple of weeks, and when I didn't get my period, I knew it had happened. I was pregnant. I had to write to Immaculate to let her know.

I thought about having an abortion, but I realized I would only get pregnant again. I needed a long-term solution. I thought of an idea. I went to see Immaculate's mother, hoping I could see Immaculate. Her mother told me she was at school and had not been to the village for a while. She suggested that I write a letter and take it to the old man at the mansion.

I had to sneak out again to go to the mansion. I was afraid that if my husband knew where I was going, he would know who gave me the tablets. In the end, I dropped the letter to Immaculate through the gate and walked away. I hoped someone would get it to her. I needed all the help I could get.

Dear Maki,

I am writing to tell you some sad news. I am pregnant. Even with all the help you gave me, I was careless and got caught by my husband. I was beaten to a pulp and the birth control pills were destroyed. I had no choice, Maki. I am contemplating abortion. I don't want to have this baby, but I am scared. What would you do, Maki? Please let me know. You are the only person I can trust. I will wait to hear from you, so please get back to me before I do something regrettable.

Your friend,
Makandida

Unfortunately, this time I did not get an immediate response from Maki, and I could not hide my stomach much longer. As it started to bulge, my husband started to be nicer and gentler to me than before. He wanted me to eat good food and would ask me many times if there was something in particular I wanted. He bought some wool for me to make baby clothes, but I had never done this before and didn't know how. In the end he paid somebody to do it for me.

I still did not say much to him, but he was much calmer. At night he would touch my stomach, talking to himself. There was less sex now, as he was scared of hurting the baby. Gradually I watched him transform into a different man.

My aunt visited once, asking if I was all right. I did not like her, and there was no point pretending otherwise. As I had no maternity dresses, I got some handouts from village women. Most felt pity for me as I was so young.

As the pregnancy progressed I got more and more scared. I knew I had to come face to face with my number-one enemy, Njaidza. I was still paying the price for her circumcision – or mutilation, as I called it – but to have her deliver my baby was another thing. If only I could go to a proper hospital! When I mentioned this to my husband, he said there was no point in travelling. Njaidza was here and would sort me out.

I was not convinced. I had more trust in modern medicine than in the traditional way. But there was no point arguing with my husband. I was to go to Njaidza's clinic. The thought made me sick.

As days turned into months I started feeling very agitated – it was a combination of fear and anger towards my husband for having made me pregnant. I knew I was not ready for a baby. But it would have to come out of me. I imagined how painful it was going to be. I couldn't feel any joy over this. I saw how happy other expectant mothers were, and how much they were looking forward to holding their babies, but I was not.

In all this angst I had a letter from Immaculate.

Dear Makandida,

I am sorry to be getting back to you so late. I did not get your letter until recently. I am sure my advice on abortion is now too late. I am sad to hear you are going through tough times. I did not realize the birth control pills would get you into trouble. I just did not want you getting pregnant before you were ready to be a mother. I will try to come over and see you. I am quite busy at the moment, but I will see what I can do. Oh, Maka, sorry I could not be there when you needed me. Good luck with everything, and I will see you soon.

Lots of love,

Immaculate

PS. I love you and miss you loads. I know you will do the right thing.

I was ecstatic. Getting Maki's letter was the best thing that happened that day – certainly better than what happened later: I started having labour pains. It was as if the baby had been waiting for Maki's letter.

My husband took me screaming in a wheelbarrow to Njaidza. By the time we got there I was drifting in and out of consciousness.

I was in labour for two days, and then the most unfortunate thing happened. I lost the baby, and by the time I regained consciousness my life had been turned upside down. I lost the baby and my husband in one day.

All I remember is feeling wet. I was lying in my own urine, because my bladder was damaged. I had what the medics called an obstetric fistula. On hearing the news of my stillborn baby, my husband had vowed not to have anything to do with me and had disappeared. He had not even waited to see how I was. He blamed me for losing the baby – he knew from the outset, he said, that I was not interested in the baby. He was sure I had put a curse on the baby before it was even conceived and therefore he considered me a murderess. As for the condition that befell me, he did not care. He thought I had got what I deserved, a punishment for my evil deeds. I was now a disgrace, and he could not have me back, ever. He had to look for another wife.

While I was recuperating, he brought my clothes to Njaidza's clinic. A few weeks later I was ready to leave. The only place I could go was to my uncle's, where I was certainly not welcome. But I had nowhere else to go. I was the smelly woman of the village. People laughed at me. I was only sixteen.

People told me there was treatment for my condition, but it cost money, and I did not have a way of earning the required amount. At least for a while I had a roof over my head – Uncle Machocho and his wife gave me a limited time to sort myself out. Once again I decided to write to Immaculate.

Dear Maki,

I am writing to you again so soon. I wish I had some good news, but it's very sad. I lost the baby, and as if that was not enough, I have this condition – obstetric fistula. It's awful, Maki. I reek of urine and I am told I can only get fixed in the city. I have no money, and without money they won't treat me. I don't know what to do, Maki. My husband disappeared and has already remarried. I am glad that at least the sexual abuse will stop now, but I might never get married again. Nobody wants me now, and I am living with my evil aunt and uncle – but only for a short time. I really don't know what the future holds for me, and writing to you helps. Do you think I should go back to school? Maybe I should. I would be happy to hear what you think.

Oh, Maki, when will you come to see us? I miss you.

Hope you get this one all right.

Your friend,

Makandida

Writing to Immaculate kept me sane. I did not get many letters back, but it was good enough for me. I also kept in touch with some of my other classmates, including Manyara, but most were now scared of being anywhere near me because of my uncle.

With my condition I had to have some hope, and knowing there were people out there thinking of me – especially Maki – gave me that. She was in a situation that none of my friends would have wanted to be in, but she had sailed through it all. We heard through the grapevine how well she was doing. When she wrote to me she was careful not to make me feel like an idiot. Her letters were always simple, but they brought me hope.

> *Dear Makandida,*
>
> *I am terribly sorry to hear of your loss. I feel bad for not having been there for you. But I can do one thing - help with the medical expenses for the condition you mentioned. I have spoken to G, and we will see what we can do. When I am ready, I will write another letter and send some money for transport for you to come over. I am sure you will be all right. The medical team at the clinic where they do the fistula repairs has a good success rate. You will be expected to stay at the clinic for the duration of your treatment, and then you will be ready to take on new challenges. We can think about school later.*
>
> *I promise you I will do whatever it takes to help. That's what friends are for.*
>
> *Meanwhile, look after yourself, my dear friend. I will be in touch soon*
>
> *Your friend,*
> *Immaculate*

The mention of medical help was the best news I had received since developing my condition. Could she really be telling the truth? I wondered what G would be thinking of all this. Immaculate was so generous, and sometimes I worried that she overdid it. Her promise to help fix my fistula made me see her in a different light. She was amazing.

I was so looking forward to seeing Immaculate, but I decided to keep this news to myself. I knew my aunt and uncle would try to stop me from getting help from someone outside the family.

Abigal Muchecheti

Chapter 22: EGIFA

Life in Zambia was not what I expected. I was not with my mother, who used to spoil me. All the time I was in Zambia, I wrote to all my friends. I wanted to know how they were doing. Society seemed to have treated a whole generation of us girls unfairly. Some got married off or accused of silly things, and some got put through some weird custom. But it was always nice to share what was going on.

A letter from Makandida left me speechless. Her having a fistula was worrying. It was a result of having to give birth before she was ready. I didn't know how I could help, but it worried me. The same week I received another letter from Immaculate. What a story. Her and G together, who would have thought it? I decided to write back to her right away.

Dear Maki,

You were right; I was smiling when I read about your romantic encounter with G. So how are you doing? How did G's wife take it? Are you at war with her?

I hope you are enjoying life. About Europe, I would not be so sure – what if G won't let you go? Oh, Maki, it must be exciting! A shame about the ngozi though. I didn't know about it. Imagine – all that time you thought ill of G, when it should have been your family. It must hurt. And Meju – how could she, miserable cow? I will kick her for you next time I see her.

I am in a relationship myself. Nothing too serious, but you never know.

Did you hear about Makandida? Awful business, Maki. Do you think she will be all right? I hope she will manage.

Stay in touch.

Lots of love,

Egifa

Abigal Muchecheti

Chapter 23: MANYARA

The circumcision was a wake-up call for me, and life was never the same after it. I ignored the pain as much as I could and concentrated on survival. Those who didn't failed to stay sane.

I was determined to challenge female genital mutilation enthusiasts, and this meant challenging my family's values and beliefs. It wasn't going to be easy, but I was determined to try. After surviving the excruciating pain, I thought I could go through anything.

When I came back from the camp my mother was not pleased by my rebellious behaviour. My parents hoped that now that I was circumcised I would settle down, and that one of the village boys whose parents were also from Malawi would start a relationship with me. Because there were not many of us sharing the same culture, relationships were expected to begin without any help. If that didn't happen, parents would always intervene. Families in the same clan became protective of daughters, and girls who married outside were abandoned by their families.

Most of my friends who were married young were not doing well, except for Immaculate. She seemed to be doing all right, but I remembered what she had written to me at the beginning.

Dear Manyara,

I hope you are all right. I know you know I did not wish to get married to G initially, and you know how much I detested him. I am ashamed to let you know I seem to have been bound to him even before I was born. The gods were waiting for me. You know this thing called culture can be a monster at times. I was never going to be able to run away from G, because the sacrificial marriage was done when I was five.

Can you imagine, Manyara? Anyway, I am trying to live for now. How are things with you?

I am happy; don't worry about me.

Miss you.

Your friend,

Immaculate

Most people did not know the circumstances of her relationship with G, but I had had my suspicions. At least she was doing what she enjoyed most – going to school. I envied her. Out of all of us forced to leave school early, she was the strongest. She managed to wrap G around her fingers. She never forgot us, but after she was married she didn't come to the village that much.

I left school after the circumcision. I could not take it. People knew when we disappeared from school for weeks that we had gone for the circumcision, and when we came back the ridicule and abuse was worse than before. In an argument, I could not justify why we did circumcision, and to me that was bad. It's important to stand up for what you believe in, but I didn't believe in it. I hated having been circumcised, and I had nothing to say in its favour, which made me angry.

"It is a mutilation of a woman's body, just admit it," one of my friends had said.

"You are evil people!" another girl, Selina, had screamed at me. "Why do you take off what God has given you? Our body is God's temple, how can you do that?"

The stigma was too much for me to bear. I was an outcast. It was as if I was responsible for my parents' actions. I already hated school, but this made it worse. I could not pass a boy in the playground who did not say, "Manyara, can I see what your vagina looks like?"

My confidence sank, and I just hated everyone at school. I screamed at my parents and my brothers. Unlike my friend Ruvimbo, who had a physical breakdown after the circumcision, I was having a mental breakdown.

Then I met Alec. He was one of those boys who lived for fun, which is why I was attracted to him. He was as wild as a bear, but we were great together, a perfect match. He was an outsider – not one of us – so I knew my parents would disapprove. I loved him, but I also found it satisfying to be going against my parents' wishes. It was my way of getting back at them for my humiliation at the circumcision.

Having a boyfriend was a challenge. Because our culture was so different from the rest of the villagers and the squatters, we were to have arranged marriages. Anyone who fell in love with someone outside the clan was considered a rebel.

My brothers had always been protective of me, and now they would not let me have any peace. They kept pushing Alec away, and I am sure if they had had the means they would have done something to harm him. They even threatened to beat him up. Luckily he was in boarding school in the city, so in many ways he was untouchable.

Alec and I made good use of the time we had together. We experimented with a lot of things, including sex. We drank and smoked a bit of weed, but nothing more serious than that. Ours was a match made in heaven because we thought alike. We did not talk about the future, though, and did not know how the relationship was going to end.

The following year, when I was fourteen, I told my mother I was not going back to school. She did not argue with me. She thought I was now getting ready for a husband. She was not happy about Alec, though. He was not a man yet, and if I was to get pregnant how would he look after me?

Life was going on exactly the way I wanted it to. That was before the decision was made to find a husband for me.

According to my brothers, I was behaving like a bitch. They thought a husband had to be found for me before I embarrassed the family. But I was set on defying them. I had had no say in the circumcision, but I was determined to have a say about who I married – and I wanted to marry Alec. Since I wanted to prove my point to my parents, I threw all caution to the wind and stopped using contraceptives. Although I was only seeing Alec during school holidays, I got pregnant when I was seventeen. So much for our experimental sex.

At first I didn't realize I was pregnant, because I did not have regular periods, which I naively attributed to the circumcision. Then I started to feel nauseous all the time. My mother was very suspicious and had a word with people from our clan. A husband was to be found for me immediately, before I brought shame to the clan and my family.

Alec was at school, and I had to let him know, so I wrote to him.

Dear Alec,

I know you will be shocked by what I am going to say. To get straight to the point, I am pregnant. I don't know what we are going to do, but I intend to keep the baby.

Please get back to me and let me know what you think we should do before my parents make plans for us.

Yours,

Manyara

He was not pleased by the news, but he knew I meant what I said. I had to wait until he came back for the school holidays to talk about things. By then I would be four months pregnant. Luckily, Alec wrote back to me immediately.

Dear Manyara,

I was not ready for a baby, but now that we are in this mess, what can I do? I hope I won't have to drop out of school, and my parents will be angry with me – but I guess that's the price we have to pay for not being cautious. I will write to my parents and let you know what they think. I am cross with you for not listening, but it's our baby.

Stay well and I will be in touch. Don't panic. I am here for you, baby. I worry about your family, though, and how they are going to react to this.

Keep smiling.

Yours,

A

I did not tell anybody that I had told Alec about my pregnancy. He was right to worry about my family's reaction – my parents were going to be livid. I could just about see their faces once they knew. In the past abortions had been arranged for people like me who fell for a man outside the clan, but I wouldn't even think of doing that. I knew that from then on I had to watch out for food that was prepared only for me. I decided to write to Maki.

Dear Maki,

My dear friend, I thought I should let you know that I am pregnant. How is my family going to take it? Imagine my father. He is going to have a fit. But I can't wait for the day. We are keeping the baby, in case you're wondering. I am scared, though, that they might give me something to cause an abortion without my knowledge. Remember Ruth in my class? She was pregnant, and because her mother disapproved of the boy, she put something in Ruth's food that caused her to abort. Unfortunately it was such a strong dose that Ruth died.

I am both scared and excited. Oh, Maki, please pray for me.

Yours,
Manyara
It was nice sharing with friends. Then the unexpected happened.

Chapter 24: BABA MANYARA

When you have children you do as much as you can to look after and take care of them.

Mine was a big family. Both wives and all the kids needed to be taken care of. My boys were doing well, but I had problems with the girls, especially Manyara. She was always a challenging child, too full of herself and big mouthed. She could say anything when you least expected it. I never knew what went on in her head.

I was so patient with her, but when she was fourteen I'd had enough. It brought shame to me to hear people talking about her and Alec. What did she see in that boy? A decision had to be reached; that relationship had to be stopped.

I needed to speak to the other members of the clan, and Mhondiwa was the person to talk to. I had to let him know that Manyara was pregnant. Manyara needed help and redemption, so hiding the facts would not help.

Mhondiwa needed time to think and to consult with other members of the clan. We reconvened in the evening, and we all agreed that enough was enough. Manyara had to be given away to a man in our clan called Manera, who had been single for a while. He was not what one would consider normal, but all the same he was a man. We did not know exactly what was wrong with him, but he was different – somewhat slow, always behaving like a kid, but good with a pencil.

What I liked about the idea was that Manyara would still have the independence and freedom she so craved. Manera did not mind that Manyara was pregnant. He liked the idea of a clever, pregnant wife.

Time was of essence, and we all knew that Manyara would not walk willingly to Manera's house. My main worry was her fury at the arrangement, but I also needed my bride price. That is what every father lives for. In the end *musengabere* – forced marriage – is the better of two evils. Honour killing, the other option, was suggested by the other members of the clan. But I could not do that to my daughter, sacrifice her in that way.

A plan was hatched to kidnap Manyara and keep her locked up with her new husband. This was done as a last resort in cases where there was no other option. I was ashamed of my actions, but how else could I deal with Manyara seeing somebody outside the clan?

It is not easy being a parent. I really wished things had not gone this far. I also blamed Manyara's mother. How could she bring up such a person? Manyara was very different from all my other children. I began to wonder if my wife had had an affair and Manyara was not mine after all. I had never seen such a personality in my family.

I had to put all that speculation aside, though. Manyara was the priority. At least the decision had been reached. I was not part of the abduction; on the day it was to take place I went away on business while other members of the clan carried out the kidnapping. A house was picked where Manyara and Manera were expected to consummate the marriage. Once that was done, everything would be all right. Manyara's child would be born within a marriage, which was dignified and proper.

Chapter 25: MANYARA

It was calm Friday afternoon and I was on my way to the school to hang around with my friends who were still there. We always met up on Friday afternoons. I was humming happily to myself, thinking of Alec. He had written after informing his parents of my pregnancy, and they were happy and looking forward to a grandchild. Alec was going to carry on with school, but we would be all right. Schools would be shut soon, and he would be back home with me. I was so looking forward to that. Being pregnant seemed to have increased my appetite for sex.

The singing birds seemed to be sharing my joy in the day. I was looking forward to seeing my former classmates. All of a sudden I heard some footsteps behind me. I was used to walking down this road, and didn't pay any attention at first. But then, before I knew what was happening, four big men covered my mouth and my face and took me away. I realized that I was being kidnapped. I could not scream, and the more I tried the more I felt like I was drowning. Then I must have lost consciousness.

When I woke, what seemed to be years later, I was face to face with Manera in a strange house. I knew Manera, but as I regained consciousness I wondered what he was doing.

"Where am I? What am I doing here?" I asked. Slowly I began to realize what was happening. My father had arranged a marriage.

Manera was holding one of his drawings and waiting for me to calm down. There was no escape. I had no idea where we were, but my guess was one of the houses in the squatters' camp. I really wanted to go home, but there was no way. I started pacing up and down until I got too tired and had to sit down. Judging by the singing birds, I knew it was dusk. We had to eat something.

Manera had been sitting and drawing, waiting for my next move. He had a talent for art. I had never paid him any attention before; he was just another village idiot to me. Some people thought he was insane. From the way he was looking at me, I knew he was making a sketch of me.

"You are drawing me, I suppose?" I said. "Make sure you get it right."

Manera smiled. I did not care what he was doing. My worry was what my father had done to me. I had always got away with saying anything I wanted, but now he seemed to be making me pay for all the things he did not like about me.

Manera was clearly not going to say anything. He seemed interested only in his drawing.

"Manera, can we talk?" I said.

"Yes, yes," he replied.

"What am I doing here?" I asked him.

He shrugged.

"Surely you didn't come here with your suitcase and drawings if you didn't know what was happening?" I asked.

Simple as he was, Manera was intelligent. He had no social skills, but he did not want to upset me by spelling out the situation. He did, though, hand me an envelope. In it was a letter from my father signed by all the family members. I realized that I was in for a shock.

In the letter, my father made it clear that the bride price had already been paid and I now had to swallow my pride for the family's sake.

Remember, the letter said, *everyone in the family will pay for your lack of foresight, so think of others in all this. For once, please listen to your father.*

What my father had failed to take into consideration was my stubbornness. I had plans for myself and my baby. The last thing I wanted was a marriage of convenience. I would rather be a single mother than spend my life with Manera. I had nothing against him, but I was not going to enter into an arranged marriage. Maybe I had ruined my life by not practising safe sex, but I believed I could still repair what was left of it.

I knew people thought I was rebellious, but it was because I have always found my parents' beliefs not only intimidating but disturbing. I wanted a normal upbringing like some of my friends had. I was not going to fight Manera or be nasty to him – after all, this was not his fault – but he was not going to have me as a wife.

I had to think of a way to get out of this godforsaken room. I thought of writing to Alec but decided against it. I did not want him failing his exams because of worry. He would know once I had fathomed how to get out of this shithole.

I decided to write to Maki, and I asked Manera for pen and paper. I wondered what Maki would think of me. I knew she would understand. I wrote as if I had my eyes closed – my handwriting could not be nice when my brain was in such turmoil.

Dear Maki,

I am in serious trouble. I have messed up my life now, Maki, haven't I? My father had me kidnapped and tried to set me up with Manera. Can you imagine, that village idiot? What would I do with a man like that in my life? All I ever wanted was marriage to a proper man – not somebody without a brain. I am stuck in a room God knows where. Anyway, I have to run away. I am not telling Alec, but I know he might find out from his parents. Maybe people now know about this. Oh, Maki, I am so cross with my father! Once I get out of this shit I will make him pay as always. Alec is still at school as you know, and we can't have our own apartment. Can you help, Maki? I know it's a lot to ask, but if you could help I would be happy. Oh, Maki, we never give you peace.

The baby is due in six months and maybe by the time we see you I will be a mother. Can you be my baby's godmother, Maki? Think about it, will you?

Till next time,

Manyara

I was desperate for Immaculate's help. But for now I had to think about Manera.

"Can I see your portfolio, Manera?" I asked.

I was asking just to be polite, but what I saw was amazing. There was one drawing that really gripped me. Manera had put our marriage on paper. He had captured my father and the group of men on the day they discussed the marriage deal. My father looked so real it could have been a photograph. The drawing was even dated and signed at the bottom.

I was amazed. I could see now how intelligent Manera was.

"Is this for me, Manera?" I asked.

"No, it is for Immaculate," he replied. I was surprised, because I did not know Manera knew Immaculate. But he knew how close I was to her, and he wanted her to know what had happened to me. I realized that Manera and I had at least one thing in common – we both loved Immaculate.

In the end, I sweet-talked Manera and managed to get the keys from him, and before long I was gone.

So much for the arranged marriage.

Chapter 26: IMMACULATE

What started as a relationship filled with tension and hatred developed into a match made in heaven. G had fallen in love with me. But though I was happy to be with him, it was not enough. I wanted more out of life. I still had not forgotten what I told my grandfather. I wanted to do my postgraduate degree in the United Kingdom. Nobody could talk me out of it, not even G. When I mentioned it to him he acted as if I had dropped a bomb on him.

"How can you do this to me, Immaculate?" he asked. "Are you not happy with me? What have I done wrong?"

"It has nothing to do with you having done something wrong," I assured him. "It's me; I just need to broaden my knowledge."

"Can you not broaden it here?" he asked.

"No," I told him, "and if you really love me, you have to let me follow my dream, G. I will be back, you know that."

"I will miss you and hope you won't be swept off your feet by some European," he said. "I would really love to marry you properly before you go, but you know it's not easy with my first wife. I am trying to sort things out, though," he told me. "Can you not wait? I want to be with you."

"I will be back, my darling," I assured him, but G was not convinced. In truth, I was not sure myself. But I was determined to do what was best for me.

I had the looks, according to people, plus the intelligence and determination to do better, but I was also in a difficult situation. I liked G, but I could not stay with him forever. He had given me what I wanted and in a way I had given him something back. I felt that going abroad would allow me to be in control of my life for once. So far I had lived my life worrying about other people, running around helping them. I wanted to be selfish for once, away from friends and family and allowed to think of myself. I needed those close to me to be responsible for their own lives for once. In a way I felt relieved to be going. I know it sounds selfish, but sometimes one has to let go.

I did not say this to anybody, but G knew. He knew I wanted to be among strangers, without worrying myself about other people. He understood and was determined to make me happy. His gift to me before I left was a party. I had always wanted to have all my friends around me before I went, and me being the person I was, 'all my friends' meant the whole village.

All the preparations were done and everyone was excited. I had invited everyone, and I wanted to remind them that they are the ones in control of their destiny. I wanted show them by my example that everything was possible. Determination was the key – and if I could succeed, so could they.

Chapter 27: G

I could not think straight when Immaculate was not with me. I could not believe how crazy I was for this woman.

She was doing well at university and was now concentrating on her final exams, which meant she did not have as much time with me as before. The little time I had with her was magical. Our age difference no longer seemed to matter at all. We were a perfect match.

I was prepared to have her at home with me all the time so that I could have her to myself, but she would not hear of it. She still had her dream. She wanted to go abroad for her postgraduate work. All this time I had thought we shared something special, but she wanted more out of life. I was worried, because I did not know how I would handle life without her.

What started as a sacrificial marriage had turned into love for me. She was all I wanted in a woman. She was fun, intelligent and we got on so well. At first I thought it was pretence on her part, but I soon realized her feelings were genuine.

If only I could have her stay close to me. I tried offering her anything she wanted if she would only stay in the country, but all she said was "I will think about it, G." I knew what that meant. What a loss.

So I had to let her go. I had kept her caged like a captive bird, and if I was lucky she would come back to me. We all hoped she would. Everyone liked Immaculate. She was generous and good to a fault, always thinking of others first. I was sure her friends and family would miss her even more than I would.

One person, though, who was happy to see her go was my first wife.

"What has got into your head, you old fool?" she said to me. "I know it's not your fault. She must be doing something to you." She thought I was bewitched. How else could a twenty-three-year-old girl drive a man in his sixties crazy? Was I not ashamed of myself?

But Immaculate had not bewitched me. She was just who she was – a lovely girl. And I could tell that she wanted me as much as I did her, or maybe that was the delusion of an old man. Perhaps, if I really wanted to, I could get Immaculate to stay, maybe by divorcing my wife and making Immaculate my princess. But it would not work. There would be repercussions if I did that. In a traditional marriage I could have more than one, but I felt torn between two worlds, the old and the new, and I could not have them both.

I was not happy that Immaculate chose England over me. I wanted her to feel the same as me. All the time we had been together I had felt revitalized, but now I worried that my world was about to collapse.

Chapter 28: MANERA

A wife – however could they think I was ready for a wife? I watched with interest while the arrangements were being made. I was to have intercourse with Manyara. What did I know of intercourse? When I was born, no one knew that I had a disability. I have heard that when I was eight months old, I had a fever and cried for twelve hours. Finally I was taken to hospital and the doctor asked my parents if they knew I was retarded.

Retarded. It was not easy for my family. Who had brought the shameful gene to the family? My parents argued, and my father threatened to leave. My mother was adamant that she would look after me, even though she knew she would be the laughing stock of the village. Mother of an idiot! What could she do?

Growing up was not easy. Attempts were made to take me to a school for the retarded, but it was too far away and my mother would not allow it. She wanted me to be with her. At the local school they laughed at me, ridiculed me and bullied me. At home my sisters were jealous because of the attention I got from my mother, who always fussed over me like I was a baby. I just wanted people to leave me alone – all I wanted was to draw. Wherever I went people talked about me, but with my drawing I was at peace.

I did not have many friends, since all the other kids found me weird – except for Maki. She used to come and spend time with me and look at my drawings. I have so many portraits of Immaculate. I liked drawing her because she was beautiful, tall and slender. She talked to me like an equal.

"Who taught you to draw?" she asked me once.

"I taught myself," I replied. It was true. I just found myself drawing things, and everyone thought I was good. I could just capture anything.

"You are so good," she said. "You could make a living at this." I was not sure about that, but she kept encouraging me. She would not give up. She even brought me paints and brushes. I am not that type of artist, though. I needed my pencil.

Immaculate was determined to find someone to help me go professional. She said she was going to talk to G about that, but my mother did not encourage it. What if those professional people took me to the city –who would look after me there?

My mother worried about what would happen to me if she died. She thought I needed a wife, but no woman in their right mind would want an idiot for a husband. I knew that because each time I tried to greet a girl she would giggle and quickly walk away from me. So when there was talk of a woman, my mother was happy. At least the woman and later the baby would keep me busy.

I did not want it, though. What would I say to Manyara? She talked a lot, and I was scared of her. Besides, a baby… I was not interested.

I did not make any attempts to be friendly. I felt she was intruding. I didn't have to worry, though, because like most women, she did not want to hang around with an idiot like me. If only it was Immaculate.

Being shut in a room with Manyara was like a joke. What exactly did they think was going to happen there? We managed to chat a little, but that was all. When she ran away I was relieved. At least I could go back to my routine.

Just after Manyara ran away my mother had a message for me from Immaculate. She always sent messages for me because I couldn't read or write. All the attempts to teach me proved fruitless. The only thing I could do was send some of my drawings to Immaculate. I knew she liked them.

This message said that she wanted all her friends to come to a party, and I was invited. I do not like big gatherings. They make me upset and bring out the worst out of me. Knowing Immaculate, I knew that the whole village would be invited, and I would be there in my own world. But she had been good to me, so I would go. I couldn't let her down. Besides, I could always draw when I was there – it would be a nice surprise for Immaculate.

Chapter 29: EGIFA

Coming back home was a great achievement for me. I could not have timed it better. I did not come back to score points, but I did want to put to shame those who had thought I was going to stop going to school. Having my family embarrassed over the so-called virginity testing had led me to work really hard. I wanted to prove a point.

My parents were proud of me. At first they had thought I was stubborn. Going to Zambia to live with my mother's relatives had not been an easy thing. My mother felt as if she had lost me and thought I would never come back to the village.

I worked so hard in Zambia. Luckily, I had great support from my uncles and aunts. I kept myself busy with my books, and my hard work was well rewarded. I never failed an examination. My grades were fantastic, and universities in Zambia fought for me. In the end I came back with an Engineering degree. My parents were so happy.

I had job offers in Zambia, but I was determined to go back home to Zimbabwe. I had my qualifications and pride to show off, and I had a wonderful boyfriend who was willing to come with me to settle in Zimbabwe. I had not allowed the old ladies to win their battle against young girls.

There were many whose lives had been messed up by these church women. I was proud of myself and my girlfriends, so many of whom had a lost youth, never to be regained.

When I got the invitation from Immaculate I was ready to shine. How could she have known I was waiting for this opportunity? That is Immaculate for you, always the mind reader.

Chapter 30: MAKANDIDA

Being rejected by my husband was the most painful thing ever to happen to me. It was not as if I cared about him, but the word 'rejection' had a special meaning for me. My parents had died and left us at the mercy of a wicked uncle and aunt. Being cast off by my husband was like the final rejection for me.

God, however, does wonders, and for me, Immaculate's help was a wonder. I had not been that close to Maki in the past, and I used to hate her for getting involved in other people's business. I came to realize, though, that her involvement was always with good intentions.

My fistula had made my life hell. I could not look for a job, not even as a house girl. Who would want me in that state? Immaculate did.

I had to go to her house in the city while she talked to G. Luckily, G never said no to Immaculate. It was as if she had cast a spell on him. Before I knew it, I was taken to a hospital that treats such conditions. I was told they might be able to help. Immaculate had given me hope and my life back. I was determined to fight. All of a sudden I wanted to live. How could I not, after being shown such generosity?

I was in the Women's Hospital for ten months. It was a very difficult time, but I had regular visits from Immaculate and even Manyara. When Maki could not visit, she wrote to me. I still have all her letters.

Dear Makandida,

I hope you are keeping well. We are all praying for you here and know you will make it. So don't give up the fight. Be strong.

I will see you soon.

Your friend,

Immaculate

It was nice to have such support. Without it I would have gone mad. My friends were determined to see me fight for my life.

Slowly I began to feel better, but I still could not walk properly. I had to use a walking stick. The leakage was getting better, but I still needed to take things easy. I was so grateful to Immaculate, who, although she was my age, seemed more mature and sensible than the rest of us.

"You have to be strong, Maka, and you will be all right," she said each time she visited me. She would sit and read me her poems, which I enjoyed. She was just amazing.

After ten months I was able to leave the hospital and convalesce at home. Maki was there to take me to her house. According to her, the only thing I needed to think about was getting better.

Thoughts of going back to school were overwhelming. I wanted to be in control of my life the way Maki was. I offered to clean for her and G to earn a little money and start saving for my education.

I started my education on a part-time basis in the evening. This helped me to start rebuilding my confidence, and I never wanted to go back to the village. My aunt and uncle wanted me to come back, but I was adamant: I was going to be in control of my life. I thought I had to write to Ranga and to my dead mother.

Dear Ranga,

How are you, my dear brother? I am glad to hear you have passed your O Level exams. I know you are worried about me, but please don't be – I am well looked after by Immaculate. All is well and I am recovering from my condition. Maybe next you can visit me during the next school holidays. It would be nice to see you again.

I have missed you so much. I hope I will see you soon.

Your sister,
Makandida

At least my brother had not lost his youth to family misfortunes.

The letter I wrote to my mother would be the last one, I told myself. Immaculate had said I should seek help instead of writing to my dead mother, but I had to write to her one last time.

Dear Mama,

You will be pleased to hear I am recovering from my condition. I do not think I will ever get married or have children, but I survived. I know you might think I am crazy – how can a 23-year-old woman say she will never get married? The truth, dear Mama, is that if I told you what I went through you would cry. People spat at me. Nobody wanted me anywhere near them. I was a burden, smelly and useless. Always soiling myself like a baby. I felt helpless lying there in bed, not able to look after myself, not able to get off the bed to use the toilet. That was suffering, Mama. I had no one to visit me except friends, no one to wipe my tears away. I cried myself to sleep every night, wishing I had never been born. The only comfort I had was to live for Ranga. Oh, dear Mama. You know there are good people in this world. If I had not met Immaculate I guess I would be dead by now. She gave me my life back, and I am so grateful.

Ranga is doing well at school and you should be proud. I intend to go back to school. That's all. I will leave for now, Mama. I may never write to you again unless there is some really good news.

Please look after us, wherever you are. I miss you so much.

Your loving daughter,
Makandida

I lost my youth when I was married off at twelve. I now had to move forward as a broken woman.

Chapter 31: MANYARA

I was looking forward to the party. I had last seen Immaculate when I lived in her house while she was at university. She had helped me get a place of my own and I was really looking forward to seeing her again.

Immaculate's desire to help others was amazing, and I do not think a single person she invited wanted to miss this party. We all knew she would have a surprise for us – she always did. I just hoped it was nothing too extreme. I did not want her to go away, but I knew that after finishing her degree she had been very agitated and had talked about going abroad.

Immaculate had been there for me and Alec when I gave birth to my boy, Alec Junior. After my escape from the ill-planned marriage my father had arranged, I needed a shoulder to cry on, and Immaculate was always there for me. She helped me financially and accommodated Alec, myself and the baby at her place in the city. G had not been willing at first to get involved, because I had run away from my so-called husband Manera, but Immaculate had convinced him to help.

She had written to me.

Dear Manyara,

I am glad you managed to stand your ground against your parents' decision to marry you to Manera. I had to convince G that you needed a place to stay until you are sorted. Feel free to bring Alec Junior to see his godmother. It will be temporary, but it will be better than sleeping in the streets. We will work something out once you get here.

Be safe, and I will see you soon.

Lots of love,

Immaculate

In the end Immaculate's house in the city became more like a mini village. Everyone who had problems thought of Immaculate, and she always had time for those in need. Maybe it was because of her humble beginnings. I felt honoured to be her friend.

I was looking forward to the party. Somehow I was sure she was up to something. I asked Makandida if she knew what was happening, but she had no idea. It would be a surprise for all of us.

Chapter 32: MARIA

Although I had no say in G's financial affairs, I did not know why he was wasting money on Immaculate. She seemed set on making us bankrupt. She was always involved in projects. The problem was my husband could never say no to her. What had she done to my husband? I heard all the excuses he made to be with her, but I kept quiet.

All this helping friends – who did she think she was, Mother Teresa? I tried to talk to G, but he got angry whenever anyone criticized Immaculate.

"G, please stop being treated like a pawn by this girl," I said to him once. "Can't you see she is using you? Once she sucks out all your money and energy she will leave you. What are you going to do then? Come running back to me?"

"See what jealousy is doing to you?" he replied. "Immaculate will not leave me, and if she does that's her choice. Besides, she is not the sort that uses people." Once we started talking about Immaculate, even it was two in the morning, he would drive away to be with her. Things were changing between us. I had known G had to have Maki but I never thought he would be so involved with her. So eventually I gave up.

I wondered what he saw in her. That's why I sometimes said he was bewitched. You never know with these modern girls. Everyone told me how lucky I was that Immaculate had not had children with G. At least the spell she put on him would slowly disappear.

All these parties and money spent on destitutes, when would she stop? Who did she think she was? No wonder her parents had nothing to do with her any more. They must have been ashamed of her.

I hated her guts, and I was happy when I heard that she was planning to go away. That served G right. Now he would come crawling back to me. Had I not said that she only wanted to use him? Thank God G would be all mine again. She would be far away and G would realize that he had lost his way. Oh, my poor man.

I decided I would go to the party and be nice. What else could I do? They always said a second wife is like a patch on a new dress. Immaculate was like that. She nearly destroyed my marriage.

I wondered if she planned to come back.

Chapter 33: THE PARTY – IMMACULATE

It was a great party – a get-together for all my friends. I was leaving it all behind. I wanted to be free of G and his money for now, his wife, my family, the girls and the village and start all over.

Everyone was there, even G's wife Maria. Finally the marriage that began in secret was now in the open. G had officially admitted to having two wives. My parents, my brothers and all the various friends I had made over the years were all there to hear what I had to say.

G had brought me a nice party dress from his last trip to Europe, and I looked magnificent in it. I was overwhelmed by the gifts he brought me; whenever he returned from a trip he would stop by the university with a present or two.

On this occasion, G chose to sit with me. His wife was with other people, and he was happy. Everyone wanted to make a speech – one by one my friends stood up to speak words of admiration for me. Some had even brought presents. I was overwhelmed by their love.

Then it was my turn to talk.

"Dear friends and family," I began, "I am very grateful to have you here. I know that some of you have left your work in the city to be here for me. It is a pleasure having you as my friends, and I thought I should share this moment with you.

"As you know, I have now finished my degree. G and I have agreed that I will go to the UK for further education. I knew that I might not get to see all of you before I left, so a get-together party was the only way. You are all invited to see me off at the airport on the 23rd of January, 1998.

"I am also letting you know that I am a godmother to young Alec. So to those of you who thought I might not come back, rest assured that I will be in Alec Junior's life. I love you all."

People were stunned, and some of my friends came over to me. Leaving? they asked. How could I be leaving? I could only smile. I was prepared to shed tears with them for now, but I really wanted to leave.

"Maki, is this some joke?" Manyara asked. "Why are you abandoning us? What will we do without you?"

"You are full of surprises!" Egifa exclaimed. "Here I have come all the way from Zambia hoping for a fresh start with all my friends, only to be told you are leaving. Why, Maki? It's not fair!"

"Will you be coming back to see us?" Manera asked shyly. Manera had a perfect gift for me. In the short period of time he had been sitting there, he had captured G and me and gave me the drawing. I was proud of him.

G was by my side pretending to be happy for me. He still thought I might change my mind about going abroad. Friends kept coming up to me, asking what they were going to do without me. I did not know what to say.

Now that I had told everyone about my leaving, the tension began to lift. People ate and drank, enjoying my company. But I had a final surprise for them. I stood up.

"Excuse me, excuse me," I said. "Before I pass you on to my lovely husband G, can I have your attention once more? I thought you would be pleased to know that my house in the city, where some of you have already been, will be turned into a shelter for abused women. I know there are women out there who have been and still are in difficult situations but cannot escape because they have nowhere to go. Now they will.

"Please pass the message on. G will help as much as he can, but we would also be happy if other people are brave and come forward to work with us. If you have any suggestions for things we can do to help these women, please talk to G. And now, before G's speech, let's all raise our glasses to a successful future for family and friends. Thank you."

There was a brief silence, then people started clapping joyfully.

Finally it was time for G's speech. He said how happy he was to have me as his wife, how proud of me he was for what I had achieved so far. He went on praising me until I felt embarrassed. Makandida surprised me by reciting a poem she had written for me. I remembered reading poetry to her while she was in hospital, but I never thought she would be inspired to write one of her own. Her poem read:

It was ten years ago when I saw her first,
A polite, humble young lady,
With a smile that you want to see again and again,

Her name Immaculate;
Her care so natural,
Like Florence Nightingale,
Like she was born a mother;
Her love so genuine,
Like she was born a lover;
Her concern so touching,
Like it's the end of the world;
Her courage so admirable,
Like she was born a soldier;
Her ways so clean,
Like a saint.
She has given us all hope,
To face and deal with tomorrow.
She is Immaculate,

"That was a lovely poem, Makandida," I said. "I appreciate it and feel honoured by it."

"I am glad you like it, Maki," Makandida said, hugging me. "I can never give you what you gave me. May God bless you, my dear friend."

I could not help but shed a tear.

It was only a few days before I would leave, and I wanted to spend my remaining days with loved ones, but I could not be everywhere. In the end I had to spend the time with G.

"G, thank you very much for caring for me and loving me," I said to him. "I will not forget you."

"Is that all you can say to a loving, caring husband?" he asked lightly.

What had started as a relationship full of hatred had ended up being a passionate one. I did not want to promise G anything, but I felt the need to make him happy. He had cared for me and looked after me and given me the opportunity to go abroad. Compared with my friends, I was lucky. I had lost my youth the day the marriage was officialized, but being married to G had given me the opportunity to turn my life around, as well as the lives of those I cared for. It was a sacrifice that had been worth making.

We went to away and enjoyed our last few days together. As the 23rd drew closer I felt excited and sad at the same time – excited that my dream was finally coming true and sad that I was leaving loved ones behind.

I was overwhelmed by the presents I got from family and friends. "What am I going to do with all this?" I asked G.

"They love you, Immaculate," G said, kissing me on the nose. "You should not be abandoning them."

Chapter 34: The End… and the Beginning

The day was bright, and the droning of aeroplanes could be heard from a distance as the minibus neared the airport. Most of my friends were there, all sad but happy for me. I was finally going to the United Kingdom for further education. My dream was coming true.

"That's it, then," I said. "I will see you all when I come back."

"That is, if she comes back," G added sadly.

"Of course she will," Makandida chipped in. "You'll think of us all the time, Maki, won't you?"

I smiled. I knew I was an inspiration, and it was good to know I had helped so many in need.

"Well, G, you know I will come back," I told him. "Time flies, and before you know it I will be back here. Besides," I added, "I will be back with you when I am on holiday."

Nobody from the village – except G, of course – had ever flown or gone to Europe, and it was exciting for one of us to be doing this. I had made the village proud. I was carrying the torch for future generations.

It was time for me to go. I picked up my bag, gave everyone a salute, kissed G, and with a smile on my face I was gone.

I was also putting on a brave face. It was painful to leave friends and family behind, but I had to do it. I had done all I could for my family, my friends and G and his family. As far as I was concerned, England was now my liberator.

I wouldn't be the wife of a dead spirit or anybody's wife and even if the spirit followed me nobody would know. I would be Immaculate. I would finally leave my family's hypocrisy behind me.

All that was left of me for people to remember was the image of the aeroplane carrying me far away from them. For me it was a new life and a new beginning in Europe.

I thought I had done Grandfather proud. And I knew he was up there, watching me sitting by the window in the *efulamachina*

Abigal Muchecheti